Mary Weatherford

Gagosian / Museo di Palazzo Grimani
Organized in collaboration with the Veneto Regional
Directorate for Museums and Venetian Heritage
Text by Francine Prose

Mary Weatherford

The Flaying of Marsyas

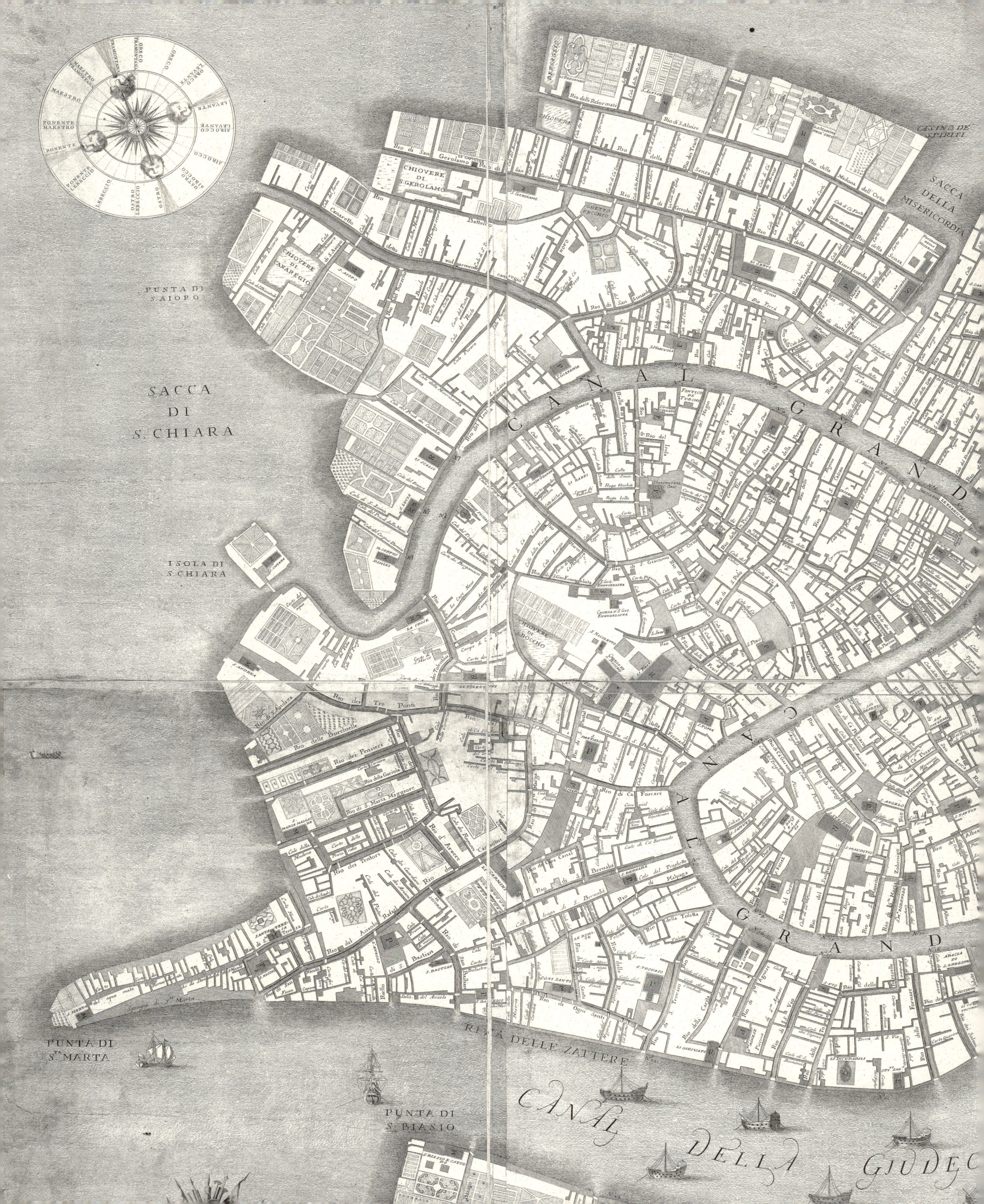

PUNTA DI S. AIOPO
SACCA DI S. CHIARA
ISOLA DI S. CHIARA
PUNTA DI Sta MARTA
PUNTA DI S. BIASIO
SACCA DELLA MISERICORDIA
CANAL GRANDE
CANAL GRANDE
CANAL GRANDE
CANAL DELLA GIUDEC
RIVA DELLE ZATTERE
CHIOVERE DI S. GEROLAMO
CHIOVERE DI CANAREGIO
Rio dei Tre Ponti
Rio delle Burchielle
Rio dei Penzieri
Rio della Gatola
Rio de S. Maria Maggiore
Rio dei Tentori
Rio della Misericordia
Rio della Sensa
Rio di S. Alvise
Rio dei Reformati
PONENTE
MAESTRO
LEVANTE
SIROCCO
OSTRO
LIBECCIO

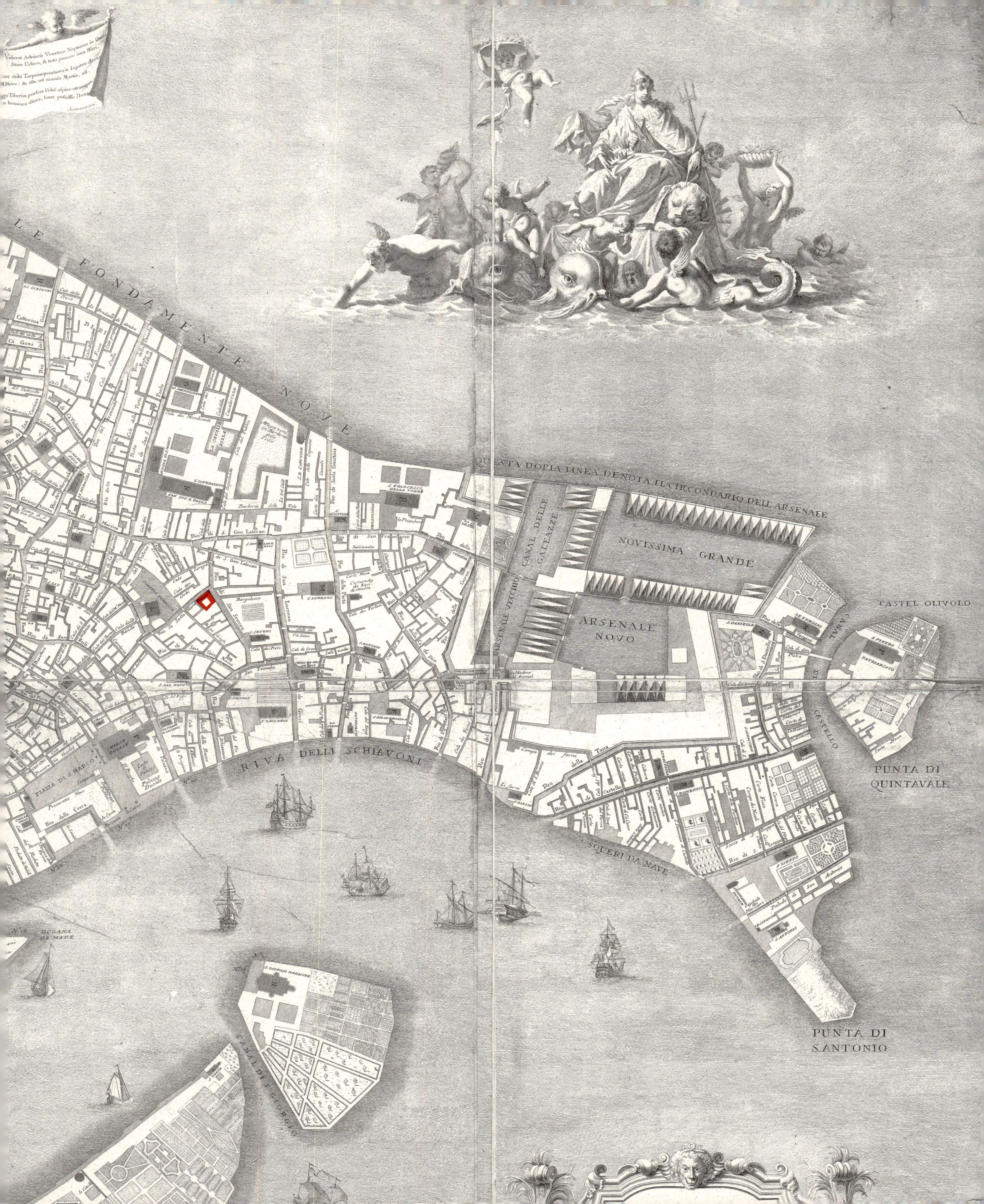

LE FONDAMENTE NOVE
QUESTA DOPIA LINEA DENOTA IL CIRCONDARIO DELL'ARSENALE
NOVISSIMA GRANDE
ARSENALE NOVO
CANAL DELLE GALEAZZE
ARSENALE VECCHIO
CASTEL OLIVOLO
PUNTA DI QUINTAVALE
RIVA DELLI SCHIAVONI
SQUERI DA NAVE
PUNTA DI S.ANTONIO
PIAZZA DI S. MARCO
CANAL DI S. GIORGIO

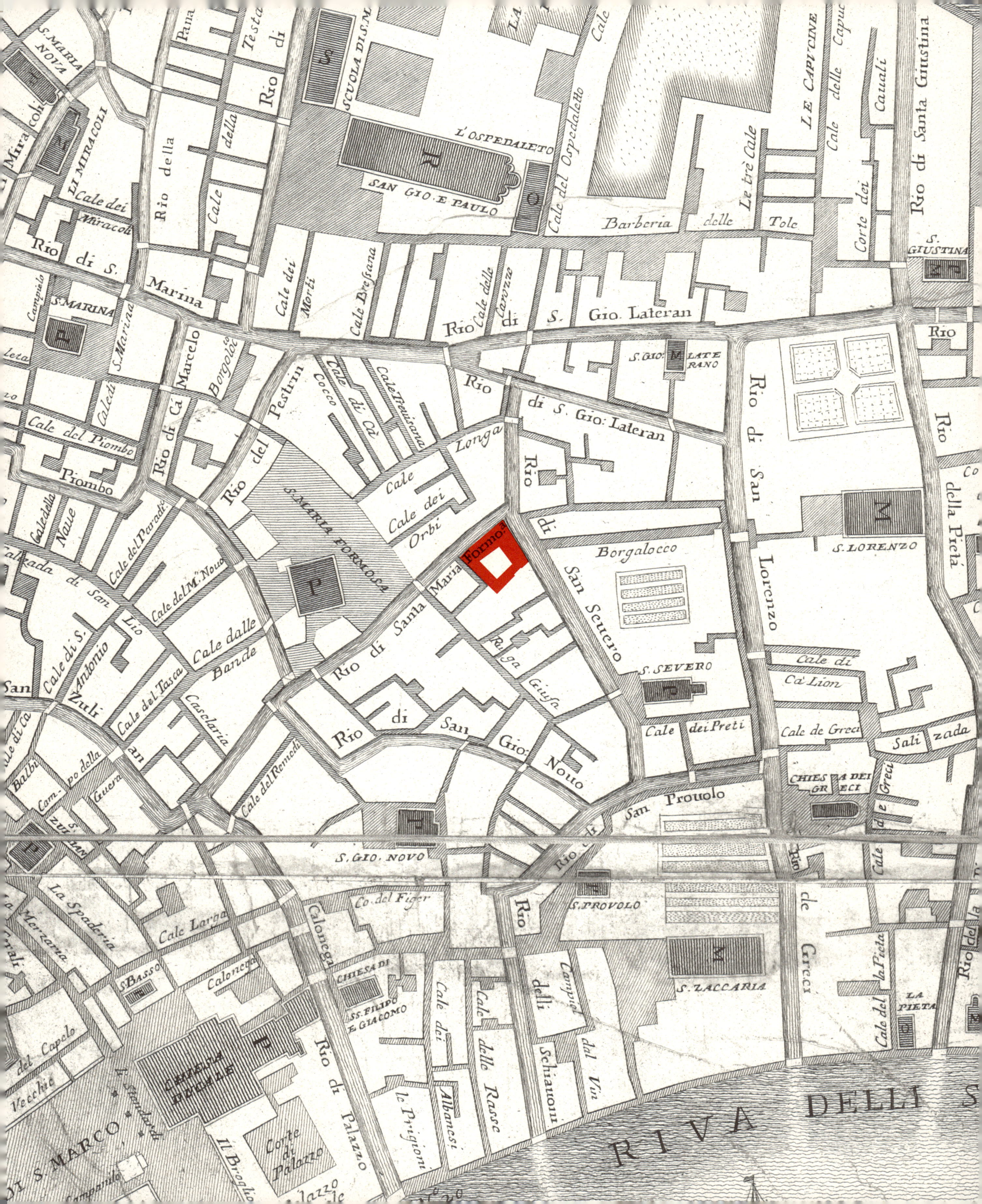

S. MARIA NOVA
Miracoli
LI MIRACOLI
Cale dei Miracoli
Rio di S. Marina
S. MARINA
Campielo
Cale S. Marina
Rio della
Cale della Testa
Rio di
SCUOLA DI S. M.
L'OSPEDALETO
SAN GIO. E PAULO
Cale del Ospedaletto
Barberia delle Tole
Le trè Cale
LE CAPUCINE
Cale delle Capuc
Corte dei Cavali
Rio di Santa Giustina
S. GIUSTINA
Cale dei Morti
Cale Bressana
Rio di S. Gio. Lateran
Cale delle Carozze
S. GIO. LATERANO
Rio
Cale Marcelo
Rio di Cà
Borgolocco
Rio del Pestrin
Cale di Cà Cocco
Cale Trevisana
Rio di S. Gio: Lateran
Cale Longa
Cale dei Orbi
Rio di San Lorenzo
Rio della Pietà
Cale del Piombo
Piombo
Rio di San Severo
Borgalocco
S. MARIA FORMOSA
Formosa
Santa Maria
Rio di Santa Maria Formosa
Ruga Giusa
S. LORENZO
Cale del Paradiso
Cale della Nave
Salizada di San Lio
Cale del M. Nouo
Cale dalle Bande
Cale di S. Antonio
San Zulian
Cale del Tasca
Cascaria
Cale del Remedio
Rio di San Gio: Nouo
S. SEVERO
Cale dei Preti
Cale di Ca' Lion
Cale de Greci
Salizzada
CHIESA DEI GRECI
Cale de Greci
San Prouolo
Rio di
Balbi
Campo della Guerra
S. ZULIAN
S. GIO. NOVO
S. PROVOLO
Rio
Co. del Figer
La Spadaria
Merzaria
Cale Larga
Calonega
S. BASSO
CHIESA DI SS. FILIPO E GIACOMO
Cale dei Albanesi
Cale delle Rasse
Campiel delli Schiauoni
Cale dal Vin
S. ZACCARIA
Rio de Greci
Cale del la Pietà
LA PIETA
Rio della
del Capelo
Vecchie
Li Standardi
CHIESA DUCALE
Corte di Palazzo
Rio di Palazzo
le Prigioni
Il Broglio
DI S. MARCO
Campanile
RIVA DELLI S

Contents

Mary Weatherford: The Flaying of Marsyas

Francine Prose

We look at lots of things that arouse our curiosity, for understandable if not always purely admirable reasons. We know why we're rubbernecking at the scene of a crash on the highway, we know what emotions we feel, but it's trickier with art. Its hold on us, and what it evokes in us, is so much more mysterious. With Mary Weatherford's work, what initially catch our eye are the bold splashes of dark or bright colors that make us rethink our notions of what color is—and isn't. We're drawn to the work by its willingness to let the material take control, by its ability to stay within certain parameters informed by art history without having to sacrifice the tawdry gorgeousness of neon, by its ability to make us reconcile something as old as the paintings on cave walls and something as (relatively) new as neon.

Why does visual art make us think about light, an aspect of the visible world that we generally take for granted except at moments—sunsets, the first day of spring, power outages—that refuse to be ignored? One reason Caravaggio affects us so strongly is not only that we know where the light in his paintings is coming from but that we can almost feel the light seeping inside us, illuminating us from within, warming us as it does so. In much of Weatherford's work there are at least two sources of light: one the ambient light reflected from the canvas and one the glowing neon tube that crosses its surface. Her paintings say to us: you can have color, you can have light, literally and metaphorically, separately and together. You can have darkness *and* light.

Weatherford's work can send us down one of those seductive and informative rabbit holes with which the Internet is pitted: the history of neon. In 1902, a French company, Air Liquide, tried unsuccessfully to market these tubes of gas for domestic lighting, but the brilliant red glow that the gas emitted failed to appeal to homeowners. Industry and the advertising business were quicker to see its potential. In 1923, a Packard dealership lit up the skies of Los Angeles with two large neon signs that attracted attention—and sold cars. For Weatherford, the story of neon is the story of modernism in America; it came from Paris, skipped New York, and went straight to California, which happens to be where the artist lives. It was in Bakersfield, she says, a town not often celebrated for much else, that she first understood the potential of those thrilling corridors of light, and fell in love with them. Her work takes its cues from cave painting, from the Italian Renaissance, from Mesoamerican art, from Goya and Picasso, but the neon reminds us: art is timeless, beyond nationality, but the fact is that we are here and now and in the United States.

If artists—Weatherford, Dan Flavin, Tracey Emin, Joseph Kosuth, Glenn Ligon, Keith Sonnier, and others—have stripped neon of its overtly proclamatory, illustrative, and commercial function, separated it from its utility and invited us to contemplate its beauty, it still remains one of the clearest markers of history and time in the urban cityscape. One need only compare photos of Times Square in the 1970s with how the neighborhood looks today to realize that the enormity of the visible change has more to do with signage and marquees than with car models, fashions, hairstyles, and crowds. By juxtaposing these strips of modernity, electricity, or science with a much older art form—paint and canvas—Weatherford affirms art's ability to span centuries, to exist both in and outside of history and time.

Weatherford's new paintings, which were exhibited in Venice, at the Palazzo Grimani, to coincide with the 2022 Venice Biennale, reinterpret the compelling and endlessly relevant myth of Apollo and Marsyas. Among all the violent, unjust, and punitive Greek legends, it is among the most extreme.

Half human and half satyr, the teacher of Orpheus and a talented musician whose instrument is the flute, Marsyas challenges Apollo, the god of music, to a contest. Marsyas will play his flute, Apollo his lyre. Which of them will be judged the more skilled and gifted artist? It's agreed that the loser will submit to any punishment that the winner can devise.

The myth comes to us with details and subplots that some storytellers have included and others have ignored. In one version, the Muses are conscripted to judge. In another, the decision is left to King Midas (already an exemplar of foolish decisions), who is punished for his loyalty to Marsyas by having his ears lengthened and transformed into the ears of a donkey. His disfigurement seems relatively mild compared to the fate of Marsyas, who—after he is determined to be the loser—is tied to a tree and flayed, his skin removed in strips.

Marsyas's mistake is to value talent over foresight and common sense. How could he not have realized that his divine opponent could sing and play the lyre at the same time, while the flute player, both hands occupied, his breath engaged in finding the perfect notes, was limited to a single instrument? In one retelling, Marsyas is doomed before the competition even begins: his flute had formerly belonged to the goddess Athena, who so disliked the unflattering way her cheeks puffed out when she played the instrument that she tossed the flute away in the forest and cursed it and whoever chanced to find it. That unfortunate soul, who must surely have rejoiced in his good luck, was, of course, poor Marsyas.

In the *Metamorphoses* (AD 8), Ovid skips the preliminary details—Midas, Athena—and goes more or less directly to the punishment. "Why are you peeling me from myself?" cries the victim, who argues that (as one might agree) a life is worth more than a flute. But the dying man's plea engages Ovid less than his agony and what the execution quite literally exposes, the interior and the secret made visible and public: blood, nerves, veins, viscera. Only when Marsyas is mourned by legions of mythical creatures, nymphs, fauns, and satyrs does the transformation (Ovid's theme, after all) occur: the dead man's blood becomes a river that flows through the Phrygian landscape.

In "The Flaying of Marsyas" (1994), the Scottish poet Robin Robertson not only shares Ovid's focus but ramps up the level of violence and gore: "The sail of stretched skin thrills and snaps/in the same breeze that makes his nerves/fire, his bare lungs scream./ Stripped from himself and from his twin: the stiffening scab and the sticky wound." Stephen Dobyns's "Marsyas, Midas and the Barber" (1986) imagines its way into the psyche of a musician whose ambition may have exceeded his talent:

> And Marsyas as he had wandered through the woods
> wondering why he had so few friends, when he saw
> the flute and picked it up, if somebody smart
> had rushed up to tell him the nature of his future
> would he have dropped the flute and turned aside?
> He was a little artist who wanted to be a big artist.
> Had he been able to see his skin nailed to the tree
> would he have denied the dancers, the cheering crowds
> in favor of a long life and anonymity forever?

And in Zbigniew Herbert's extraordinary poem "Apollo and Marsyas" (1961), the satyr's cry of agony is itself a kind of music. Apollo is unmoved, but the witnesses to his death suffer along with him: a nightingale drops to the ground, frozen, and the hairs of the tree to which Marsyas has been tied turn white all at once in the wake of his death.

In general, myths privilege magic over logic, yet this one may strike us as particularly illogical. Why would the satyr agree to such a risky bargain? Why is his punishment so extreme? Others have suffered for excessive hubris, for insulting or thwarting the gods, or for rejecting their sexual advances. Guilty of stealing fire, Prometheus is chained to a rock and doomed to have his liver devoured by an eagle, a torture repeated daily for eternity. But mostly these transgressors'

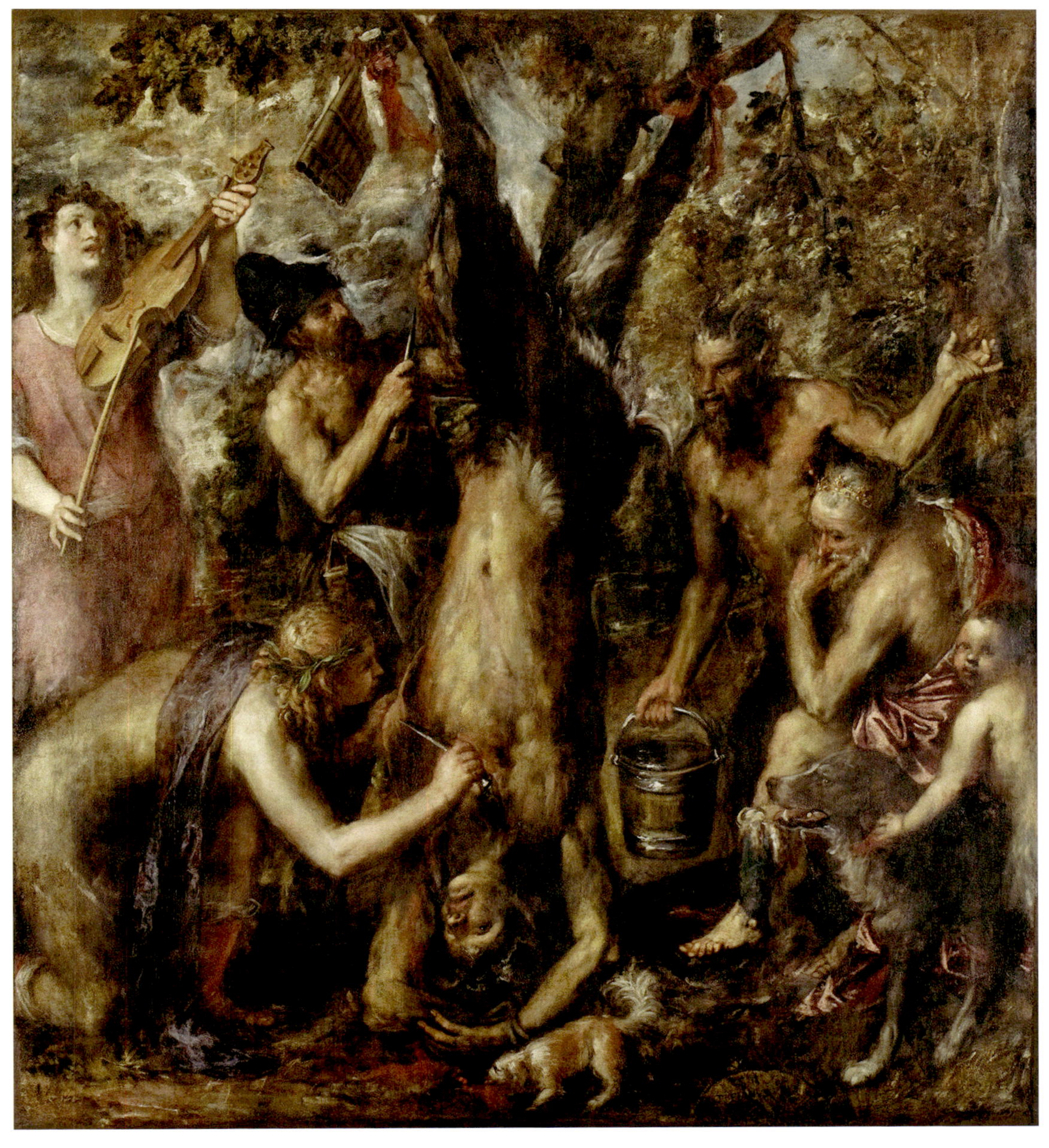

Fig. 1
Titian, *The Flaying of Marsyas*, c. 1570–76
Oil on canvas, 86 5/8 × 80 1/4 inches (220 × 204 cm)
Olomouc Museum of Art–Archdiocesan Museum Kroměříž, Czech Republic

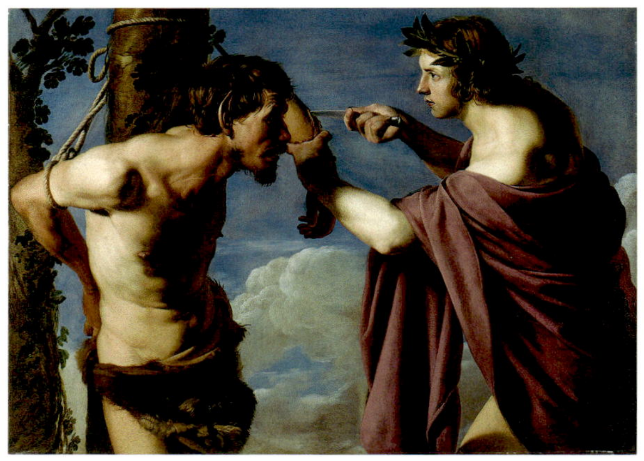

Fig. 2
Bartolomeo Manfredi, *Apollo and Marsyas*, 1616–20
Oil on canvas, 37 5/8 × 53 5/8 inches (95.5 × 136 cm)
Saint Louis Art Museum. Friends Fund Endowment and funds given by
Mr. and Mrs. John Peters MacCarthy, Phoebe and Mark Weil, and Christian B. Peper

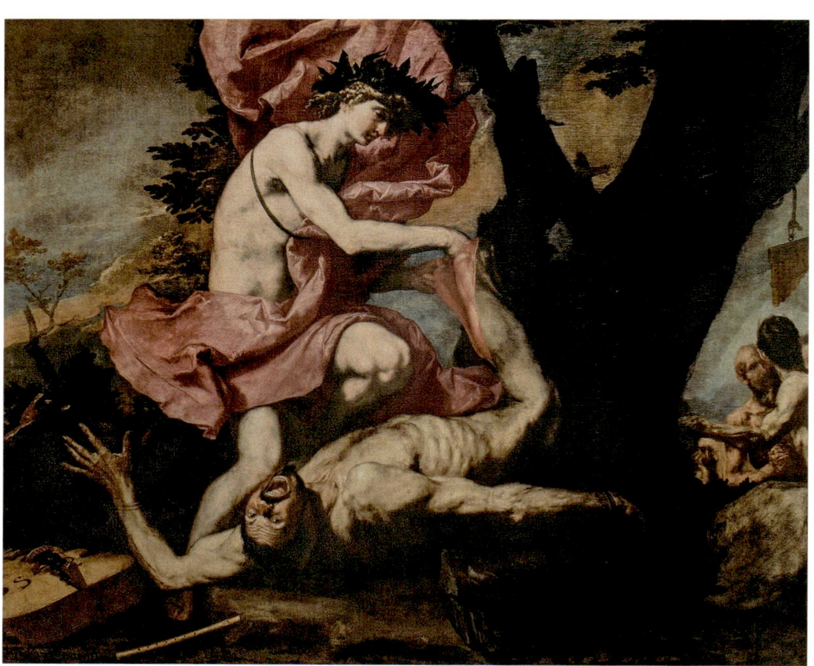

Fig. 3
Jusepe de Ribera, *Apollo Flaying Marsyas*, 1637
Oil on canvas, 79 1/2 × 100 3/8 inches (202 × 255 cm)
Royal Museum of Fine Arts of Belgium, Brussels.
Acquired from J. et A. Le Roy, marchands, Brussels, 1899

sentences involve transformation rather than torture; being turned into a calf or a flower surely seems preferable to having one's skin peeled off in strips.

Why, then, does the myth continue to fascinate poets and painters? What is it saying to us, and to what are we responding? Is it simply one more variation on the familiar story of hubris punished, of the cruel and imaginative ways in which mortals have been made to suffer for daring to challenge the power of the gods? Is it warning us against the kind of blind faith that seduces us into danger? Is it telling us that—to paraphrase the last words that Ovid has Marsyas cry out—human life is worth more than a flute: the classic answer to the question of whether the masterpiece or the old woman should be rescued from the burning museum?

What's striking is the fact that Marsyas is front and center in the visual and verbal narratives that have been fashioned from his sad story. If he emerges as the hero (however misguided) or at least the center of these retellings, are we meant to conclude that he is the one with whom the poet and the painter not only sympathize but identify: the artist who believes so strongly in his work that he is willing to suffer and die for it? Something about the legend may remind us of Franz Kafka's story "The Hunger Artist" (1922); suffering is its hero's art.

The mystery—and the drama—of the myth inspired Titian, whose painting *The Flaying of Marsyas* (c. 1570–76; fig. 1) has provided a more direct inspiration for Weatherford's new work: a fittingly Venetian source for paintings destined for exhibition in Venice.

Titian has never failed to speak to us, but his voice—amplified by the 2021–22 exhibition of his mythological paintings at Boston's Isabella Stewart Gardner Museum—has never seemed louder or more clear. Maybe it's because these paintings are so violent, because they find such ineffable beauty amid the disorder and chaos that we feel so strongly, closing in around us, at the present moment. It's hardly coincidence that, though Weatherford saw the Titian painting in a show at Rome's Quirinale in 2013, she filed the idea away—and then began to work on these paintings on January 7, 2021, the day after the one on which we watched the sort of bloodlust that Apollo is sating erupt in our nation's capital. This possibility suggests an underlying truth that runs from Titian through Weatherford and is certainly present, most strikingly, in Herbert, who lived in Poland under the repressive restrictions of the Eastern-bloc dictatorships and was obliged to employ covert and metaphorical (but no less subversive) ways of addressing political violence.

Of all the pictorial representations of the flaying of Marsyas made during the Renaissance and Baroque eras, Titian's is by far the most bloody-minded, the most (in every sense) unsparing, and the least aestheticized. Other artists portrayed Marsyas at the moment before the torture begins, or immediately after it has begun. His skin is still intact, almost flawless, and his body is often almost shockingly beautiful as he prepares to meet his fate. In Bartolomeo Manfredi's *Apollo and Marsyas* (1616–20; fig. 2) the god holds a knife, threatening the bound musician, who seems to have just realized what horrors lie ahead. In Jusepe de Ribera's 1637 canvas (fig. 3), the satyr is splayed diagonally across the lower half of the canvas; his face is contorted in agony—the god, again grasping a blade, appears to have begun his barbaric labors on the lower half of the musician's body—but at least for now, most of Marsyas's flesh is still intact. The knife so prominent in these works is almost hidden in Titian's painting, so that we have to look for it, and we find it with a shock that intensifies the sense of nightmare.

By the nineteenth century, the horror and the bloodshed have essentially been sanitized, vanished from Marsyas's story. In Elihu Vedder's *Young Marsyas* (1878; fig. 4) the musician is restored to his Arcadian fantasy world and to his flawless boyish beauty; sitting under a tree, naked in the snow, he plays his melodic tunes for an enraptured audience of bunnies. Only Titian takes us farther into the story, past the point at which there is only the mangled corpse to remind us of what has just occurred.

Lucian Freud described Titian's mythological scenes as possessing the "little bit of poison" that every great painting requires. He speculated that the poison in the Titian paintings may be "a sense of mortality." But if Titian's *Diana and Actaeon* and *Diana and Callisto* (both 1556–59) possess that drop of poison—the venom of mortality—*The Flaying of Marsysas* strikes us as having been steeped in it. The painting is the scream that Herbert transmuted into song. Dating from the 1570s, it is one of Titian's last works, painted in his old age, when we can assume that mortality would likely have been at least intermittently on his mind.

I can't think of another painting that so brilliantly depicts the ways in which horror can exist in the midst of great beauty. Hanging upside down, the dying Marsyas cleaves the painting down the middle. He's half man, half meat. But Apollo, crouched in the lower-left-hand corner as he painstakingly goes about the work of flaying Marsyas, looks so pretty, so cherubic in his laurel wreath and blond curls, we can hardly believe that he is the same deity who ordered this grisly execution. It's a party, a social event. A cute little dog is licking up Marsyas's blood. What a treat! There's even live music: an angelic creature is playing the violin. There are spectators, among them a child. The old man watching the execution is said to be Titian's self-portrait. The convergence of great beauty and great violence in Titian's painting is partly why the work was so beloved by the British philosopher and novelist Iris Murdoch, who wrote about it in three of her novels. In an interview with the BBC, she spoke of the painting as having "something to do with human life and all its horrors and terrors and misery, and at the same time there's something beautiful, the picture is beautiful, and something also to do with the entry of the spiritual into the human situation."

The paintings in Weatherford's series *The Flaying of Marsyas* (2021–22) address the complex ways in which time has worked its influence and its magic on Marsyas and on Titian. The story is still in there, hidden

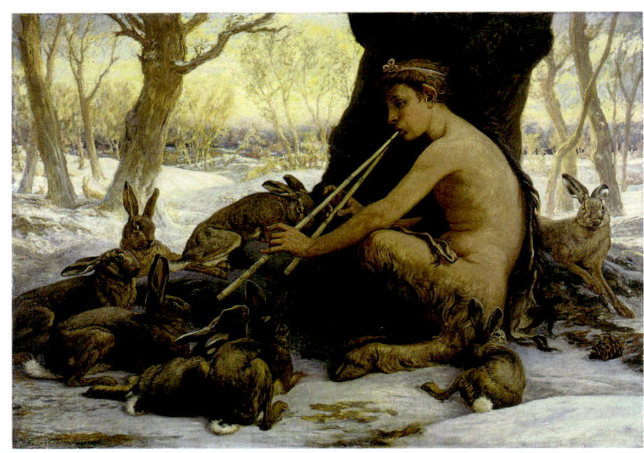

Fig. 4
Elihu Vedder, *Young Marsyas (Marsyas Enchanting the Hares)*, 1878
Oil on canvas, 37 1/4 × 53 3/4 inches (94.6 × 136.5 cm)
Crystal Bridges Museum of American Art, Bentonville, Arkansas, 2013.7

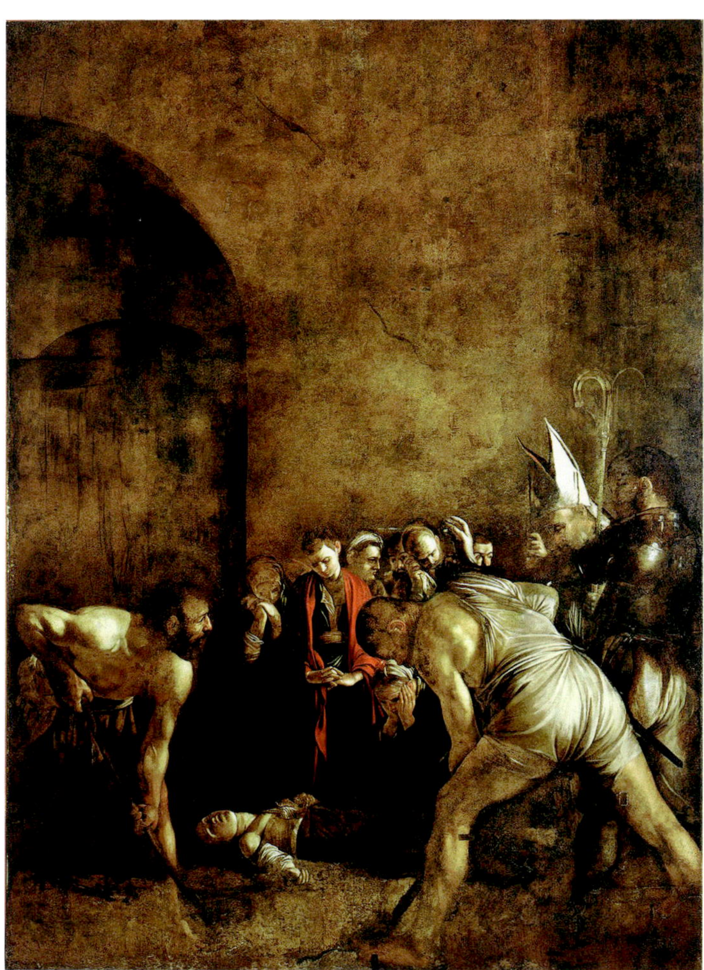

Fig. 5
Caravaggio, *Burial of Saint Lucy*, 1608
Oil on canvas, 160 5/8 × 118 1/8 inches (408 × 300 cm)
Chiesa di Santa Lucia al Sepolcro, Syracuse, Italy

within these new works, but we have to search for it. If we look long and hard enough, or alternately, if we let our eyes drift out of focus, the little dog will pop out at you, and look! There's Apollo, over there. Like Titian, Weatherford feels free to give us areas of mystery and darkness; she too makes us intensely conscious of background and foreground. The dark, empty negative spaces that Titian embeds in the scene throw the central action into greater relief; Weatherford's neon tubing creates a brilliant scrim of light that separates us from the areas of darkness merging on the canvas.

We want light to illuminate the scene we are viewing, but the neon that Weatherford has chosen—in both its harshness and its beauty—suggests that this is not precisely the mediating and inviting glow that we might have wished for. In fact, it's painful to stare too long or too closely at the neon rod, reminding us that light cannot save us, no more than art could save Marsyas. Like Titian, Weatherford alerts us to the strange and unpredictable operations of fate. How could Marsyas have known—how could anyone have known—what cruel destiny would befall him when, with perfect confidence, he began to play his flute?

Another thing that art can do is make you see something that you didn't see a minute ago. It's a source of primal pleasure when something comes into focus. Weatherford has credited, among her influences, a 2009 show at the Grand Palais, Paris, *Une image peut en cacher une autre* (One image may hide another), a major exhibition of works containing hidden images—from the faces Arcimboldo constructed from fruit and vegetables in the sixteenth century to the bodies that emerge from Edgar Degas's Normandy landscapes. It reminds us of the joy we felt as children when we first saw images that popped into focus when we unfocused our eyes, the pleasure we still feel when we look at a painting by Hieronymus Bosch and see something morph into something else—a metamorphosis that, no matter how often we've seen the painting, we've somehow never noticed.

I can remember being told, probably in college, that you weren't *supposed* to see things in, say, a Jackson Pollock painting. But Weatherford's work makes you think: why not? Isn't it a human impulse to try to find something concealed inside something else? And why should we deny that impulse in the service of fine art? How many of us—I'm including myself—can recall the profound and joyful shock of first seeing, as children, the vintage trompe l'oeil print of the two fashionable ladies at tea (or are they sipping ice cream sodas?) that, on second glance, reveals the skull at its center?

Speaking of Caravaggio's light, the color of these paintings recalls the vast expanse of darkness at the top of his *Burial of Saint Lucy* (1608; fig. 5), a chasm of brown that seems lit from within. Weatherford speaks of warm earth tones, and they're certainly here, but one doesn't evoke *The Flaying of Marsyas* and go toward browns and deep reds without having the viewer think, as Titian so clearly thought, about the flesh beneath the fragile and terrifyingly vulnerable protection of skin.

I suppose you could say these are dark paintings. I suppose you could say that it's a dark moment. As I write this, war is raging in Ukraine, and as we watch it unfold, on television and on social media, each of us becomes a version of Titian's self-portrait: a spectator at a tragedy.

Weatherford's works call to mind Goya's black paintings, Picasso's *Guernica*, and of course the Titian. Complicated, cautionary, dark, they nonetheless remind us of what art has the capacity to do: to reflect the world around us, in both its horror and violence and its beauty and grace. Human beings can not only destroy but create, and those creations are, as time has shown, what (we can only hope) will survive and endure.

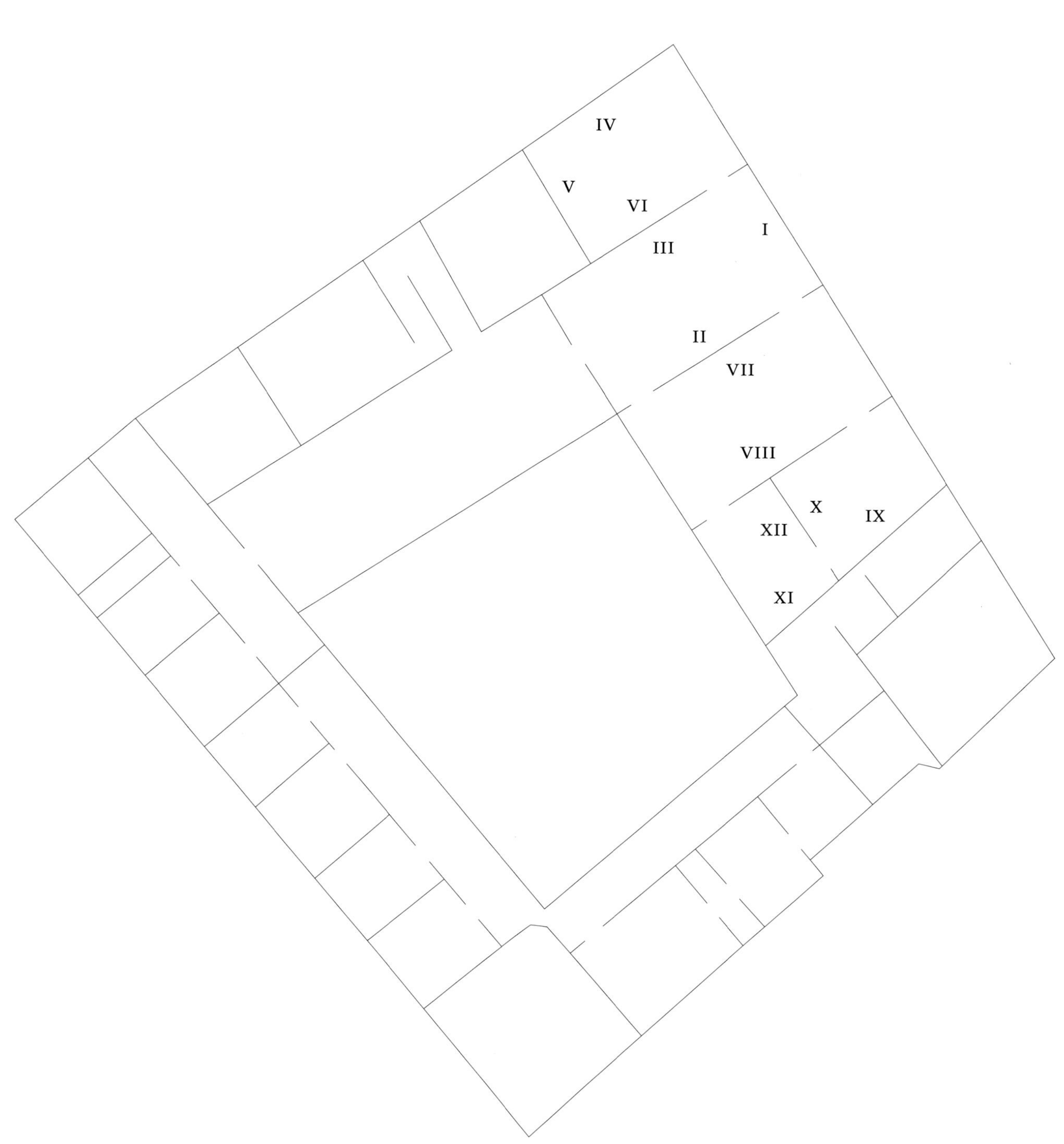
IV
V
VI
I
III
II
VII
VIII
X
IX
XII
XI

Museo di Palazzo Grimani, Venice
April 20–November 27, 2022

Exhibition design by WHY Architecture, Los Angeles

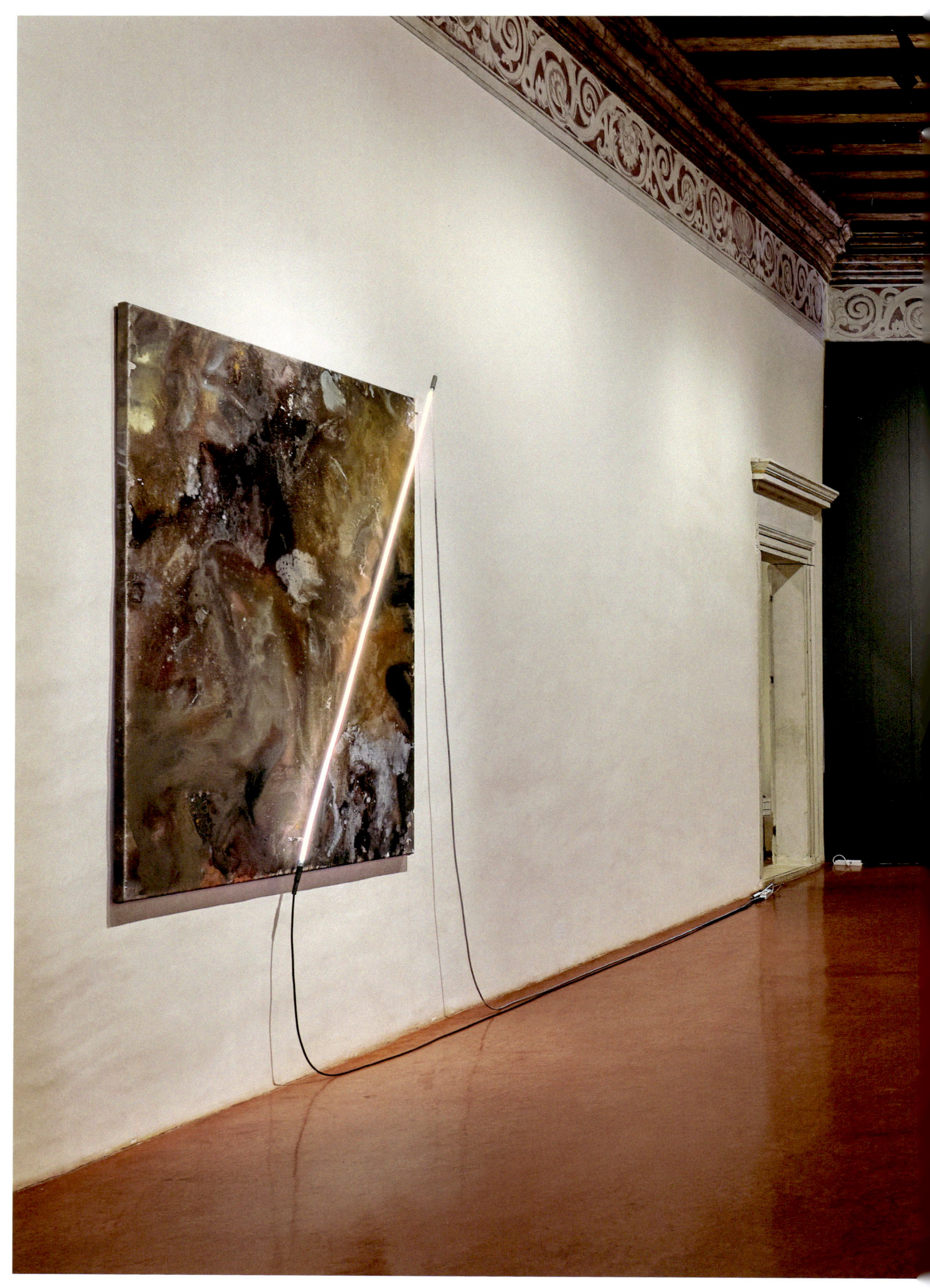

III

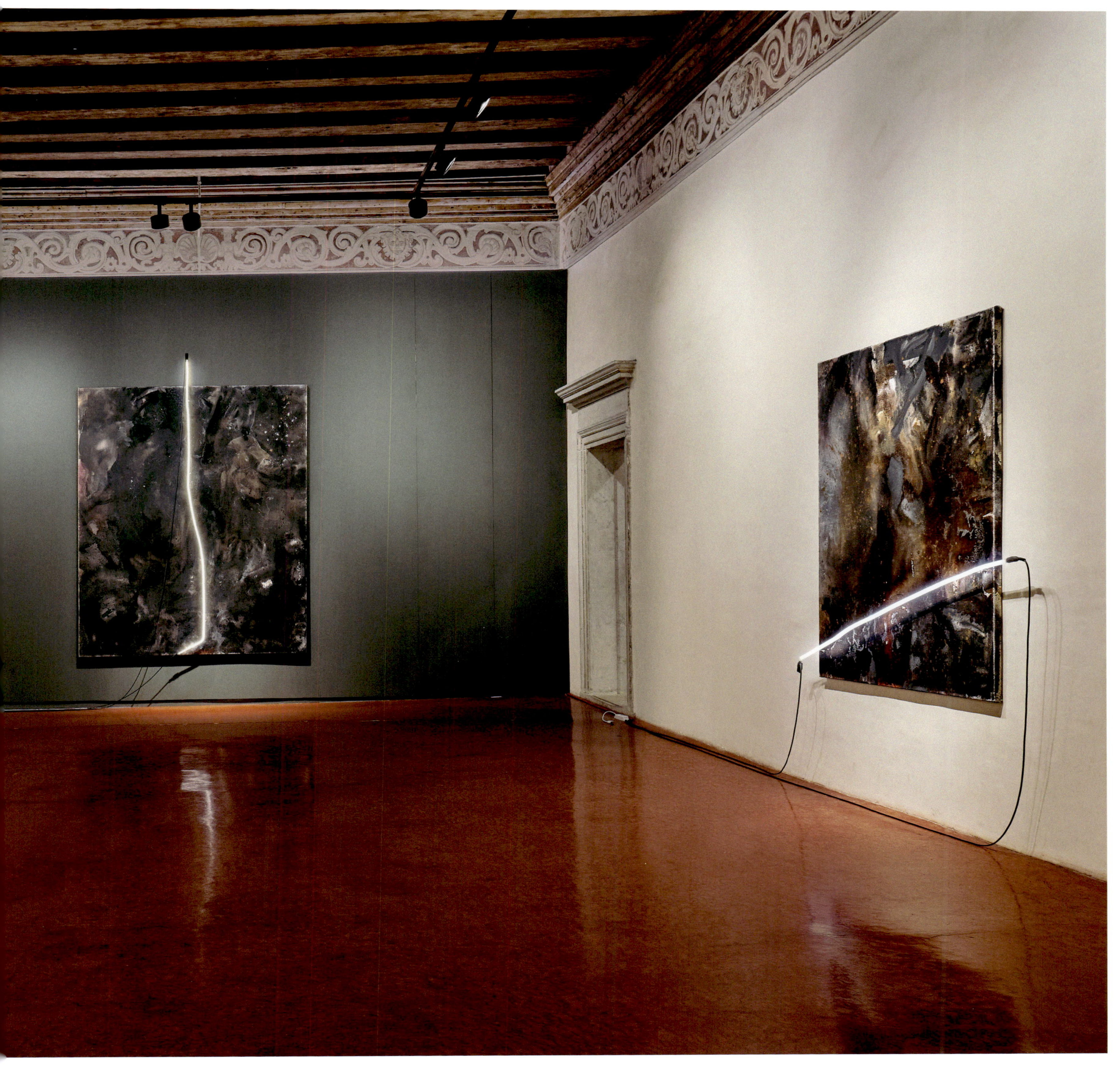

I

II

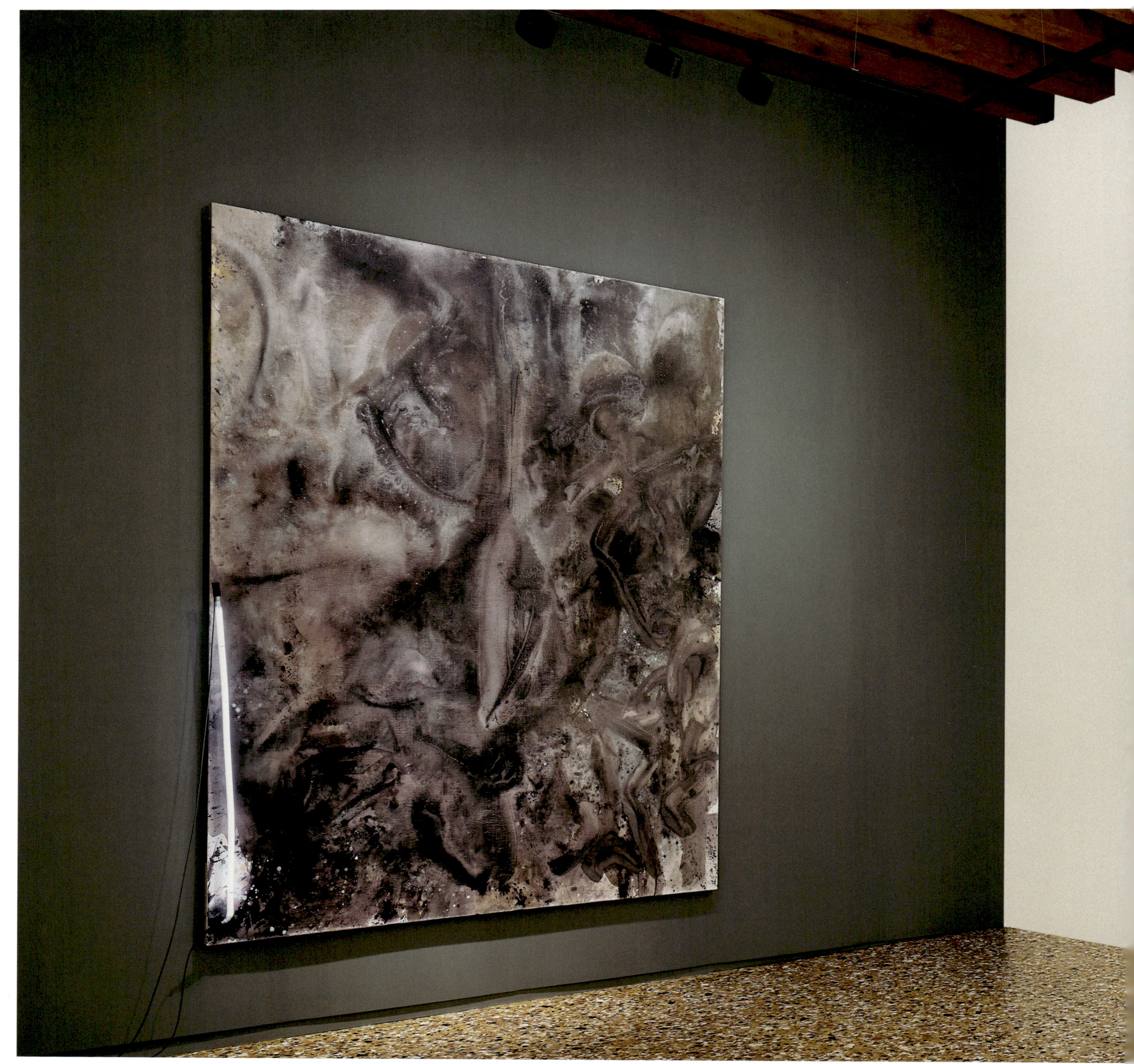

V

IV

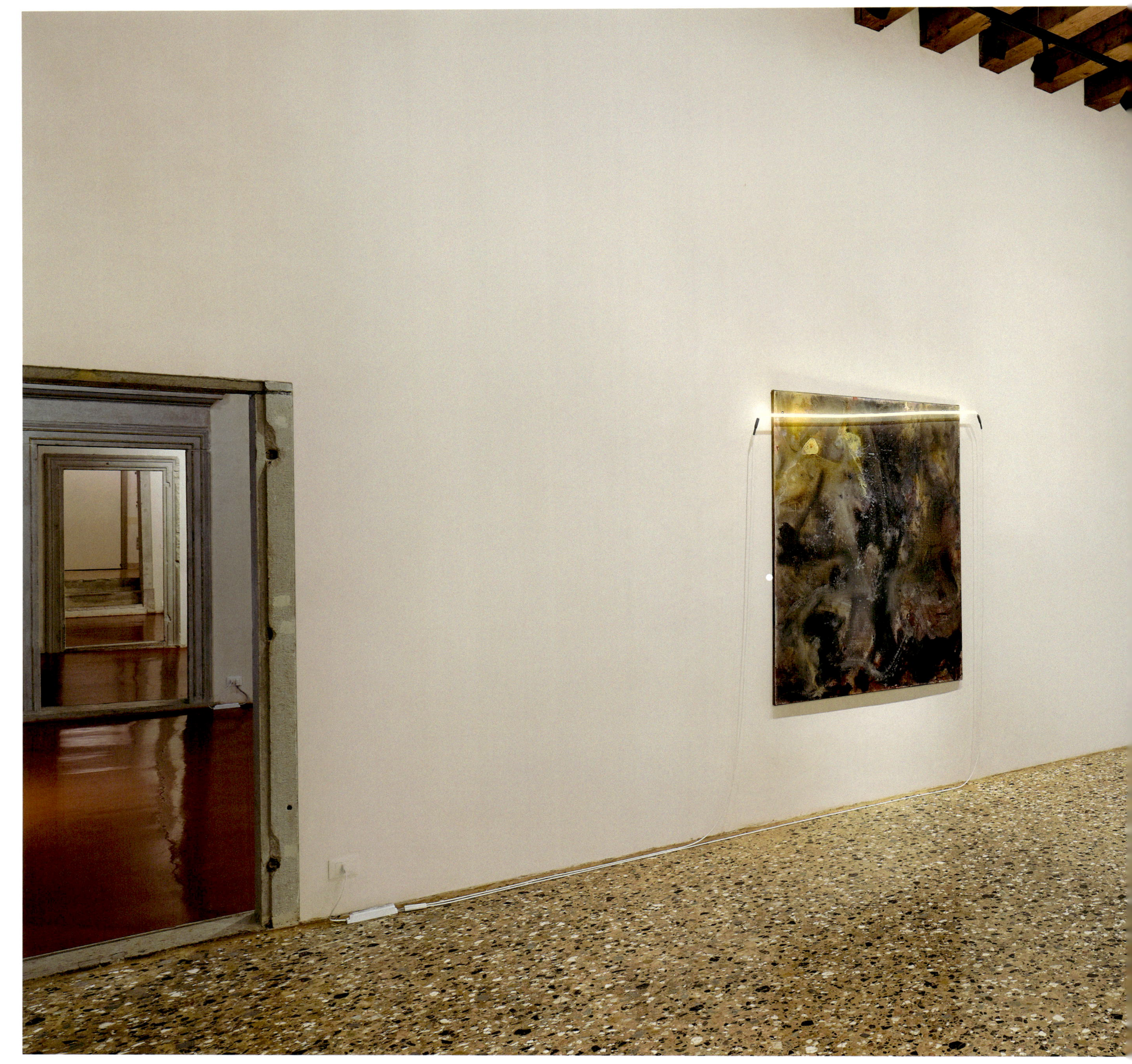

VI

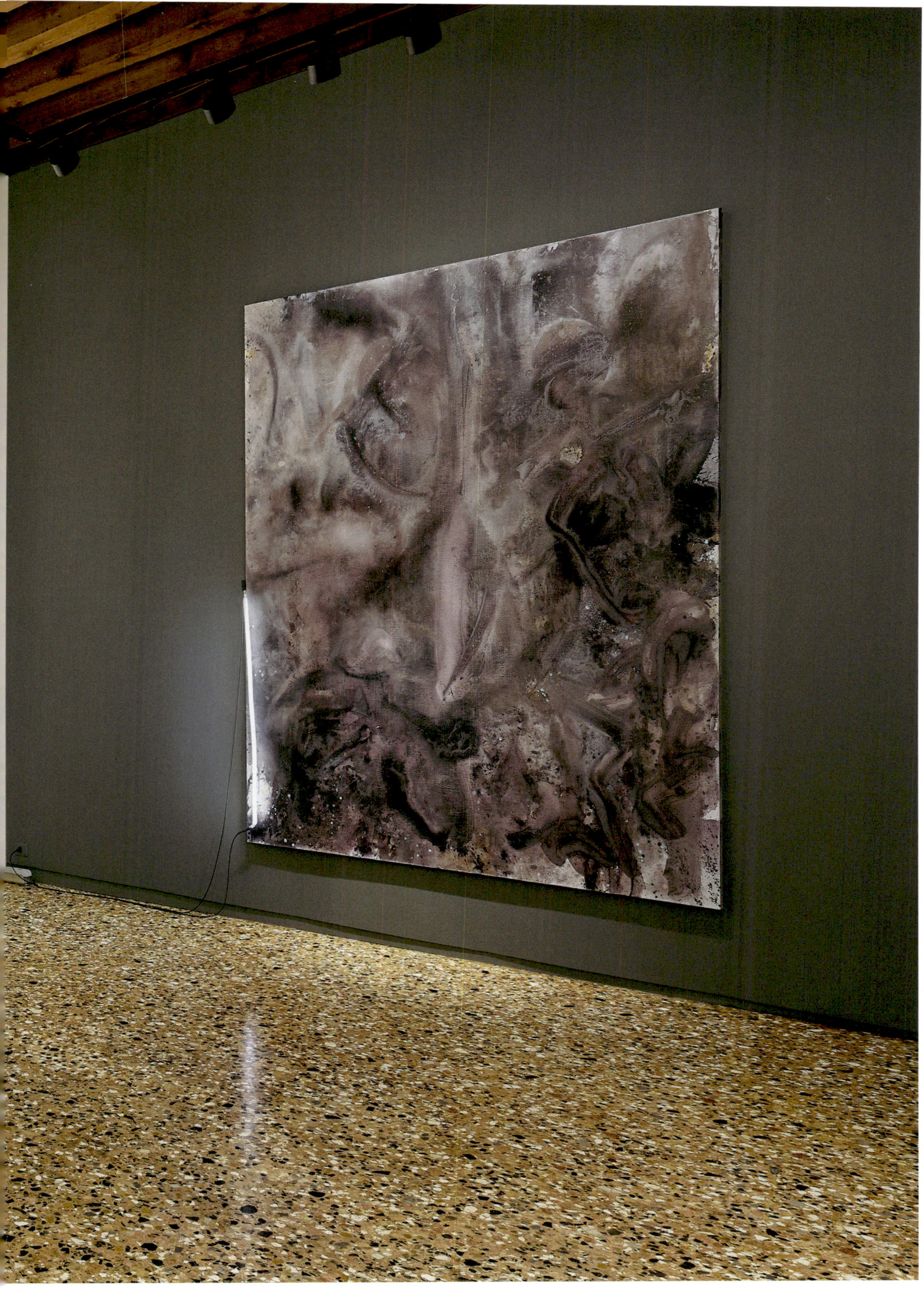

V

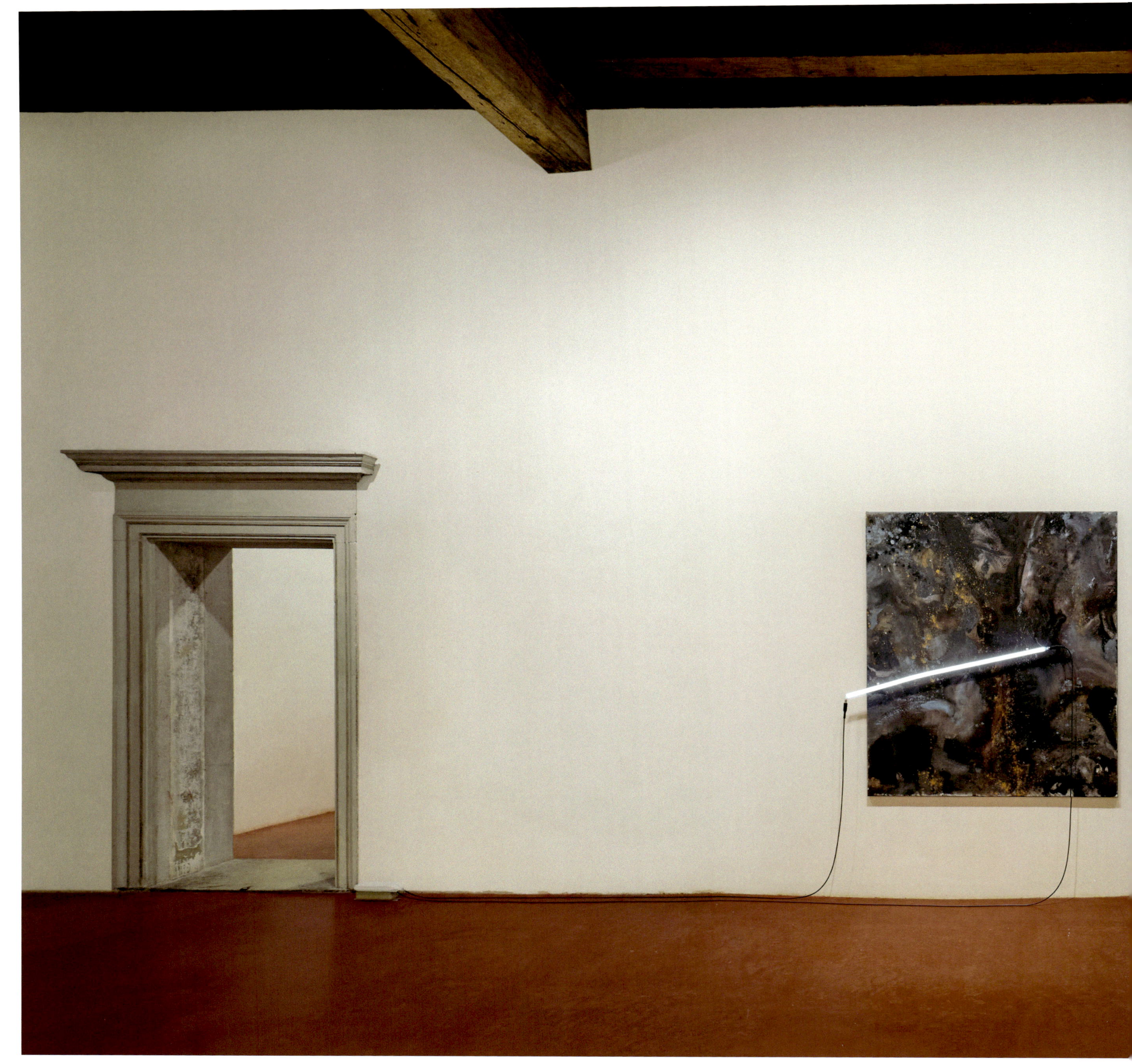

VII

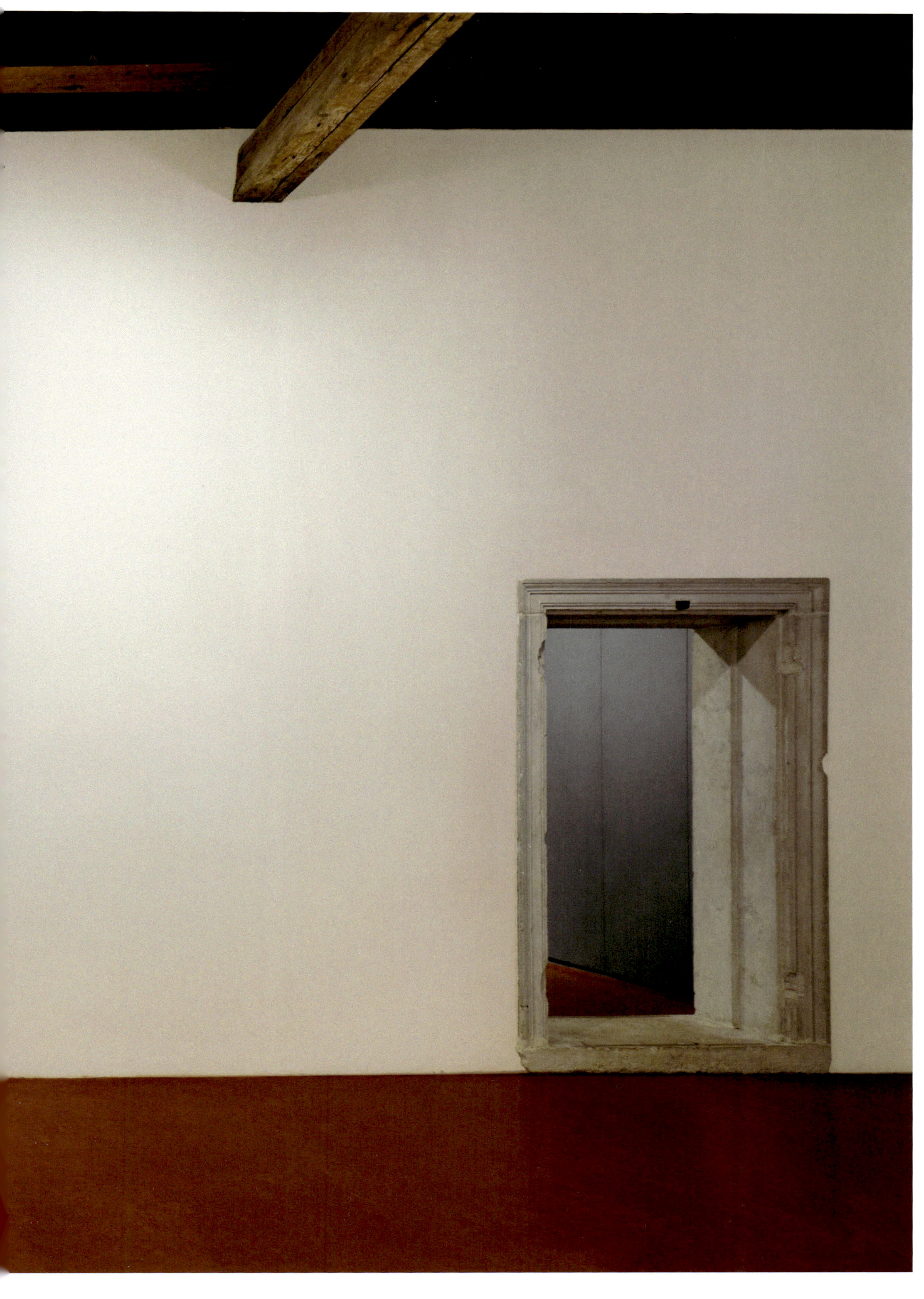

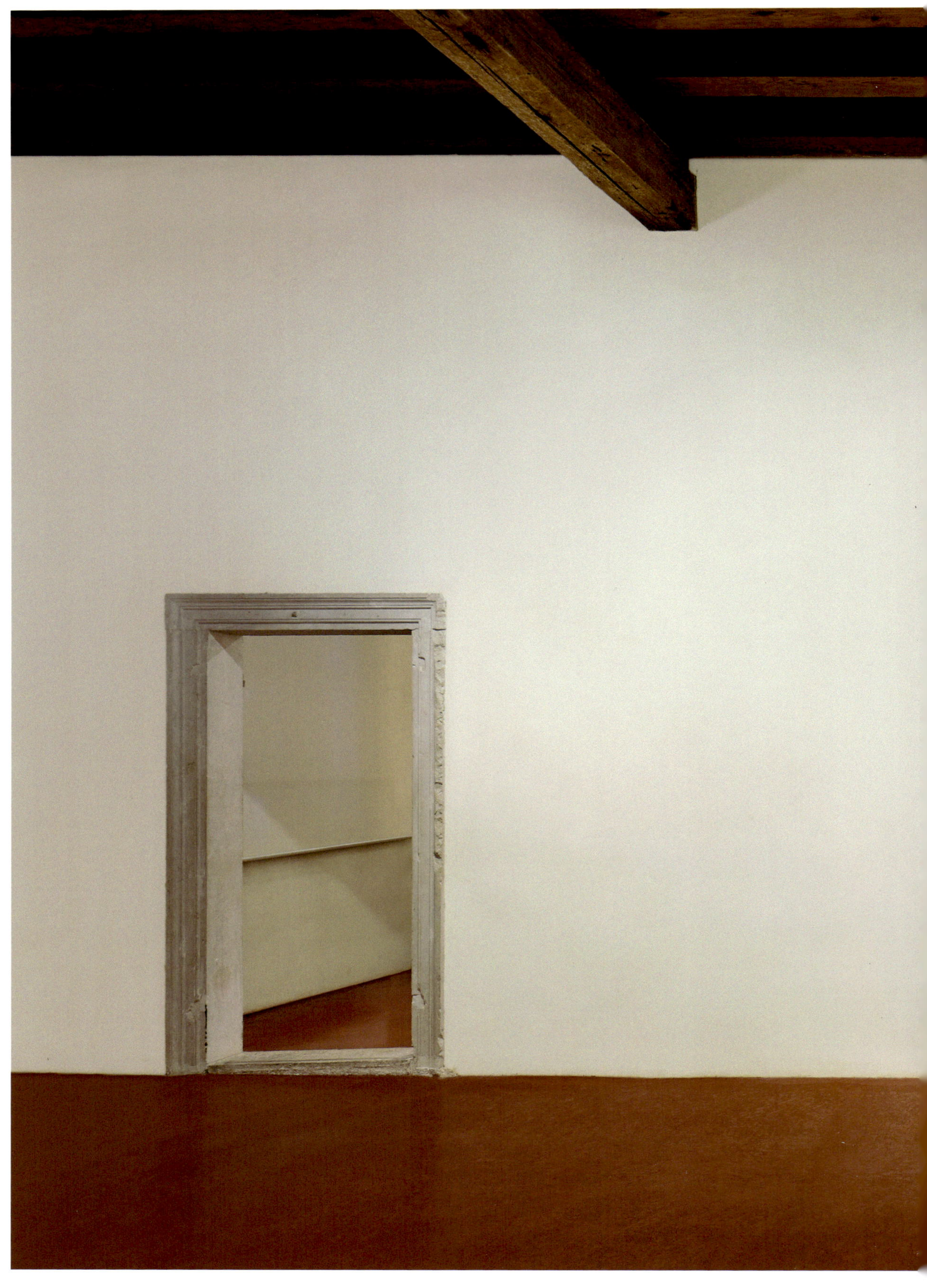

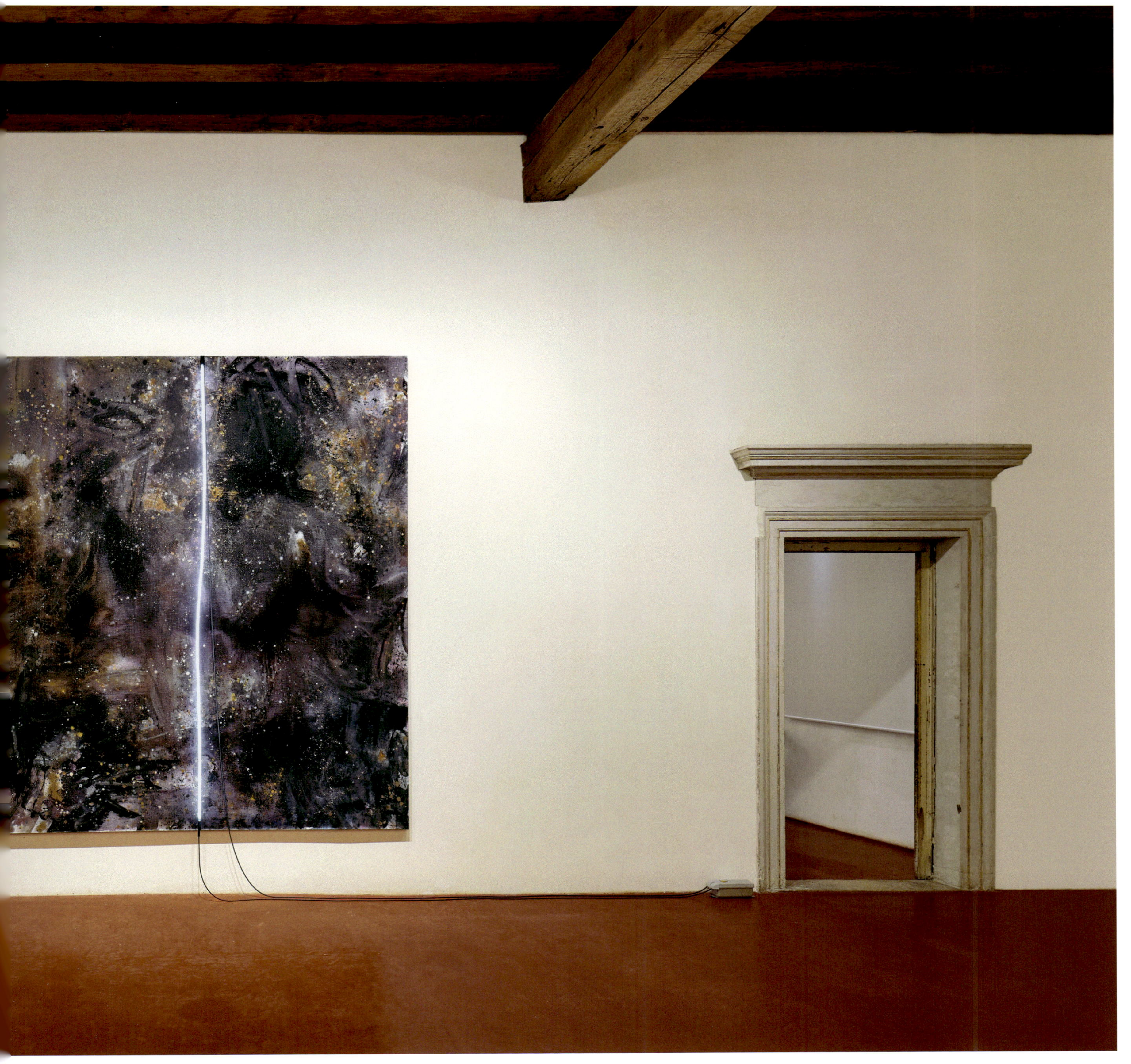

VIII

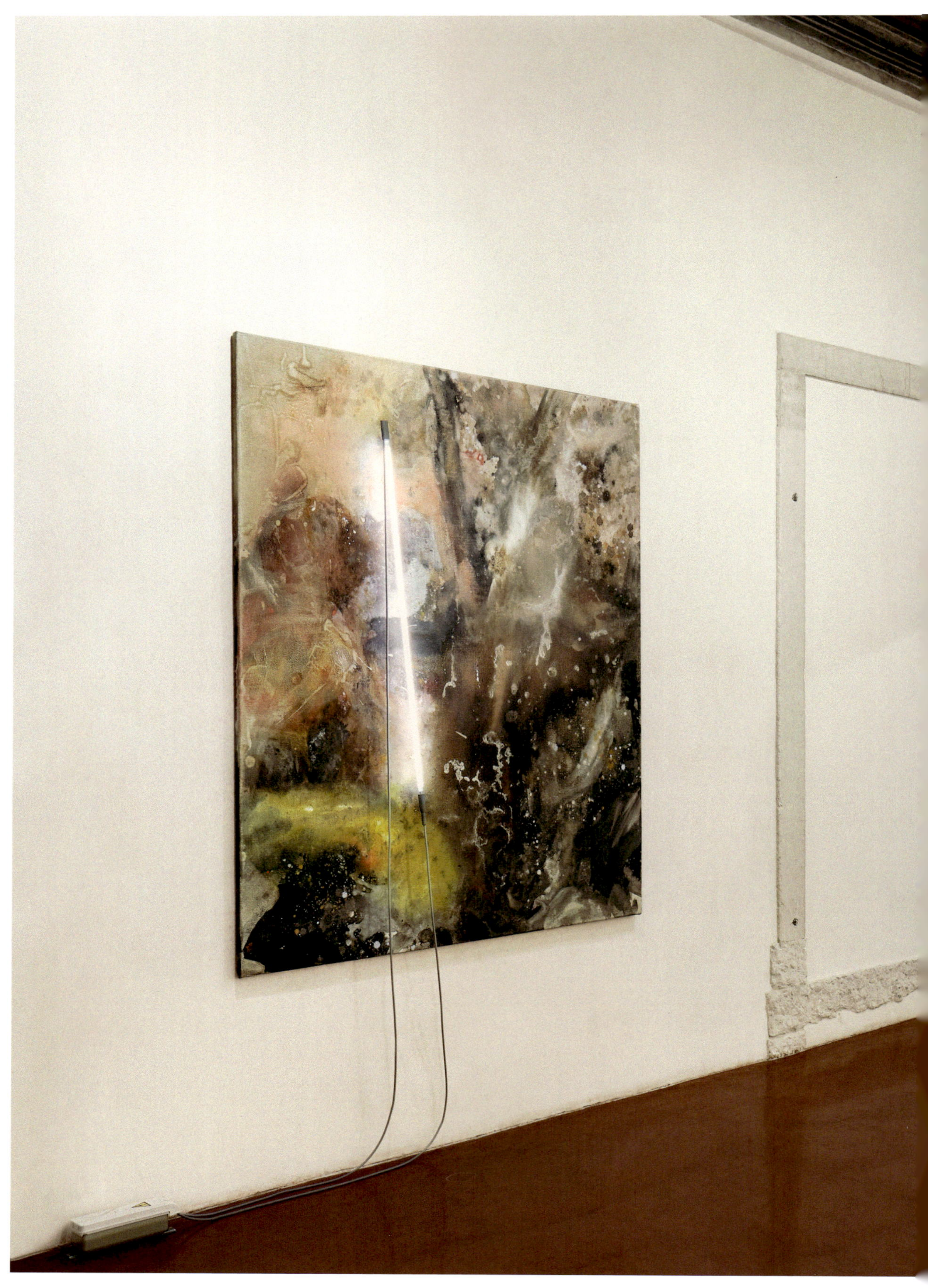

IX

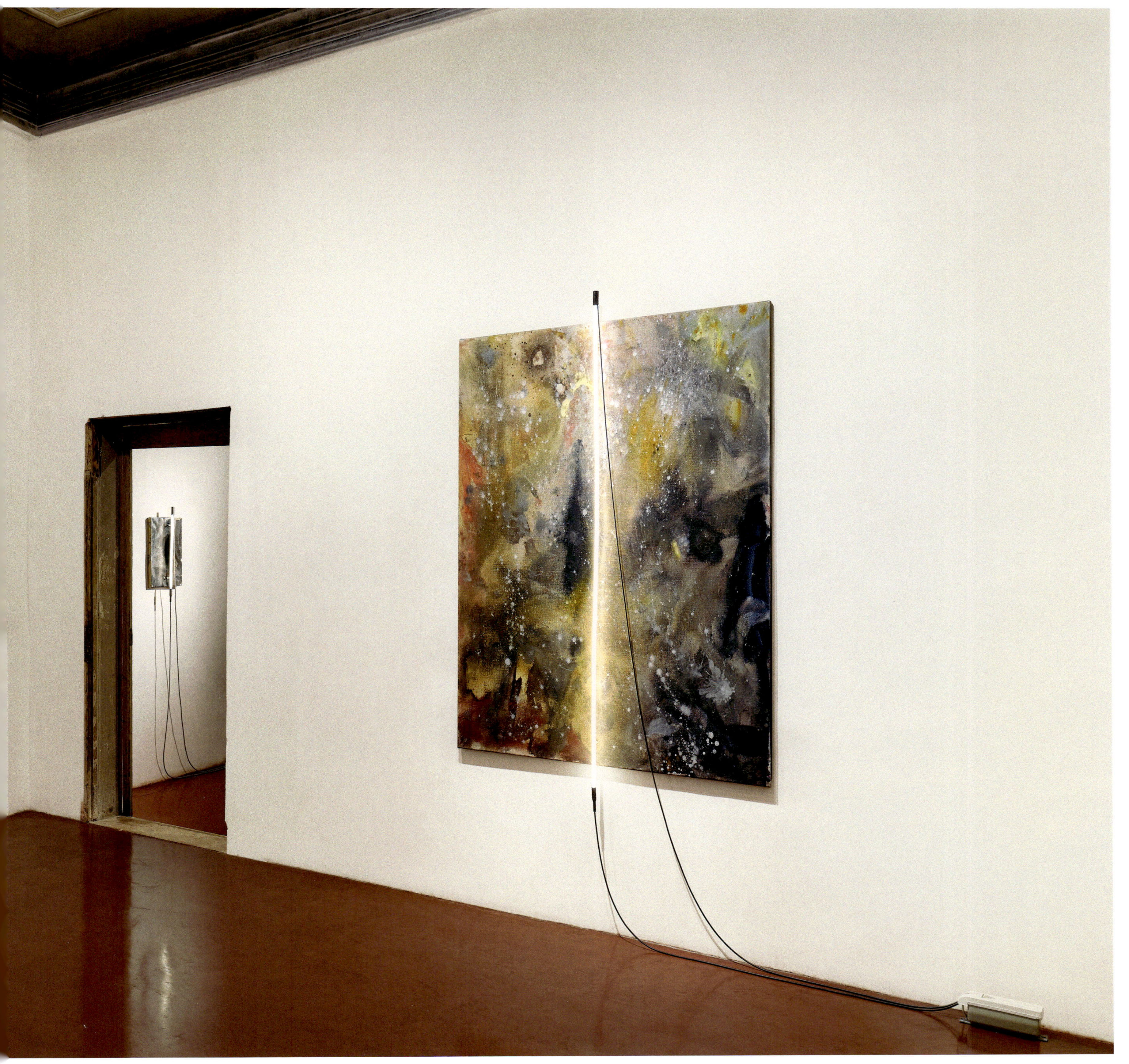

X

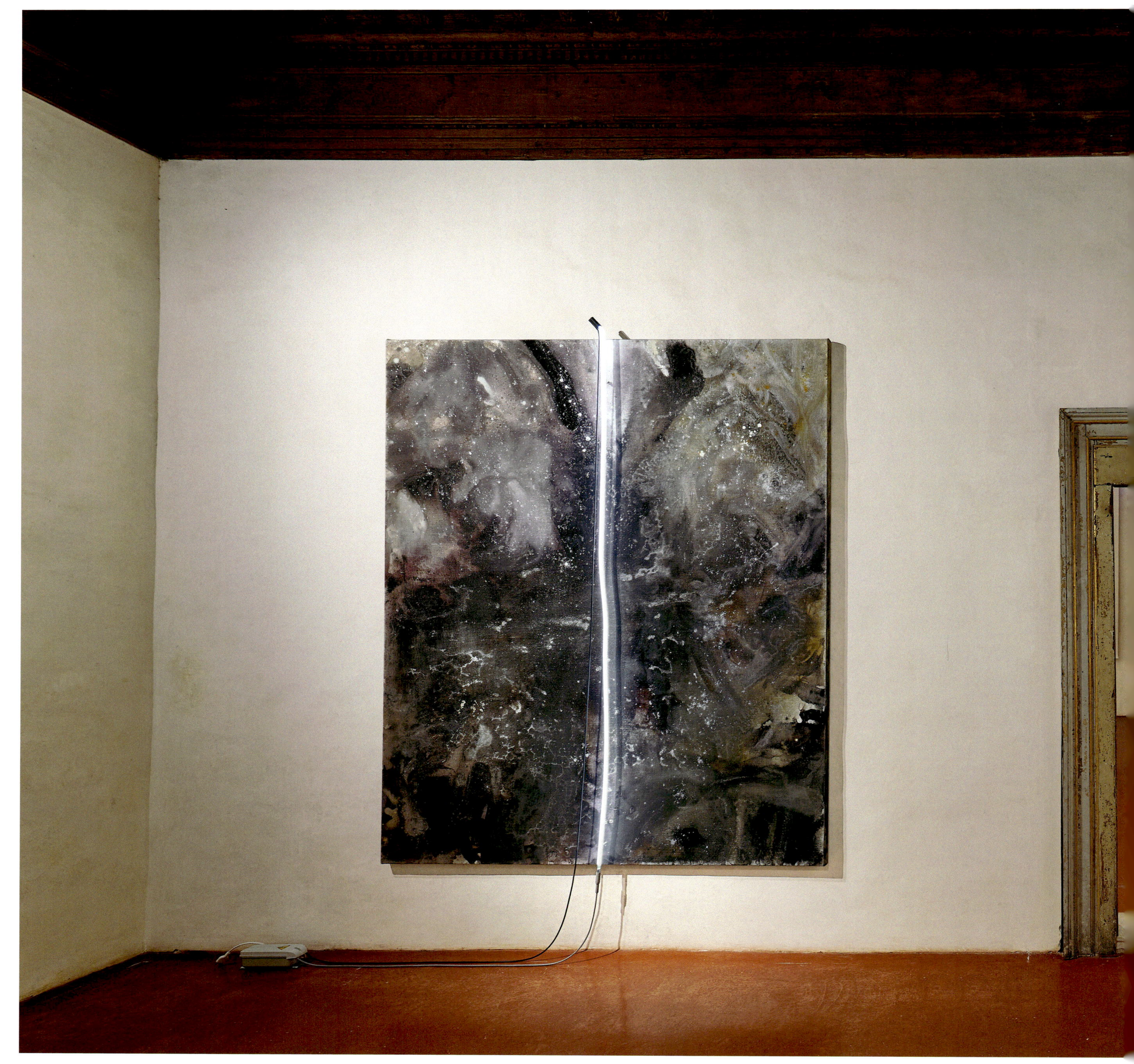

XII

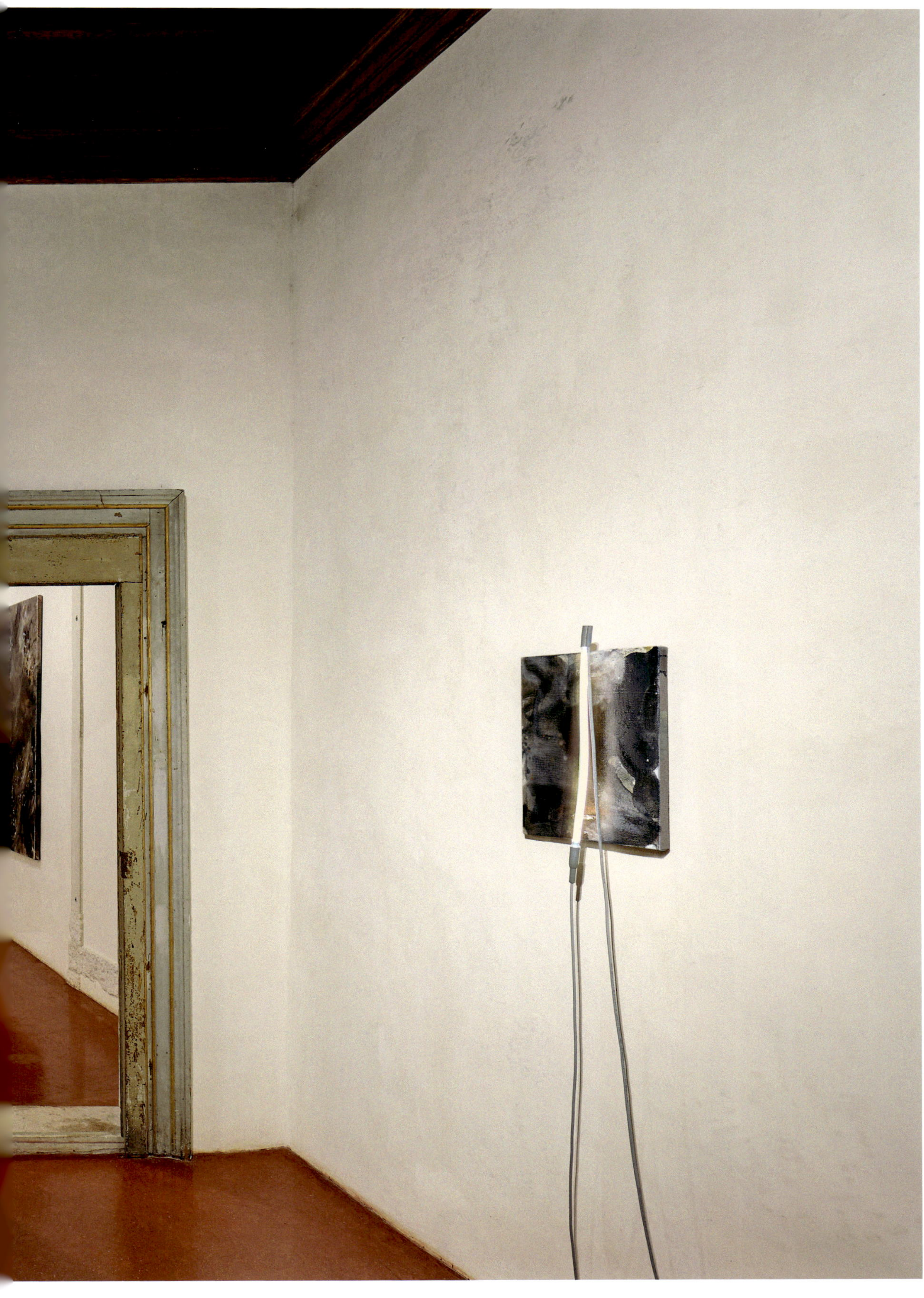

XI

Plates

1 *The Flaying of Marsyas—4500 Triphosphor*, 2021–22

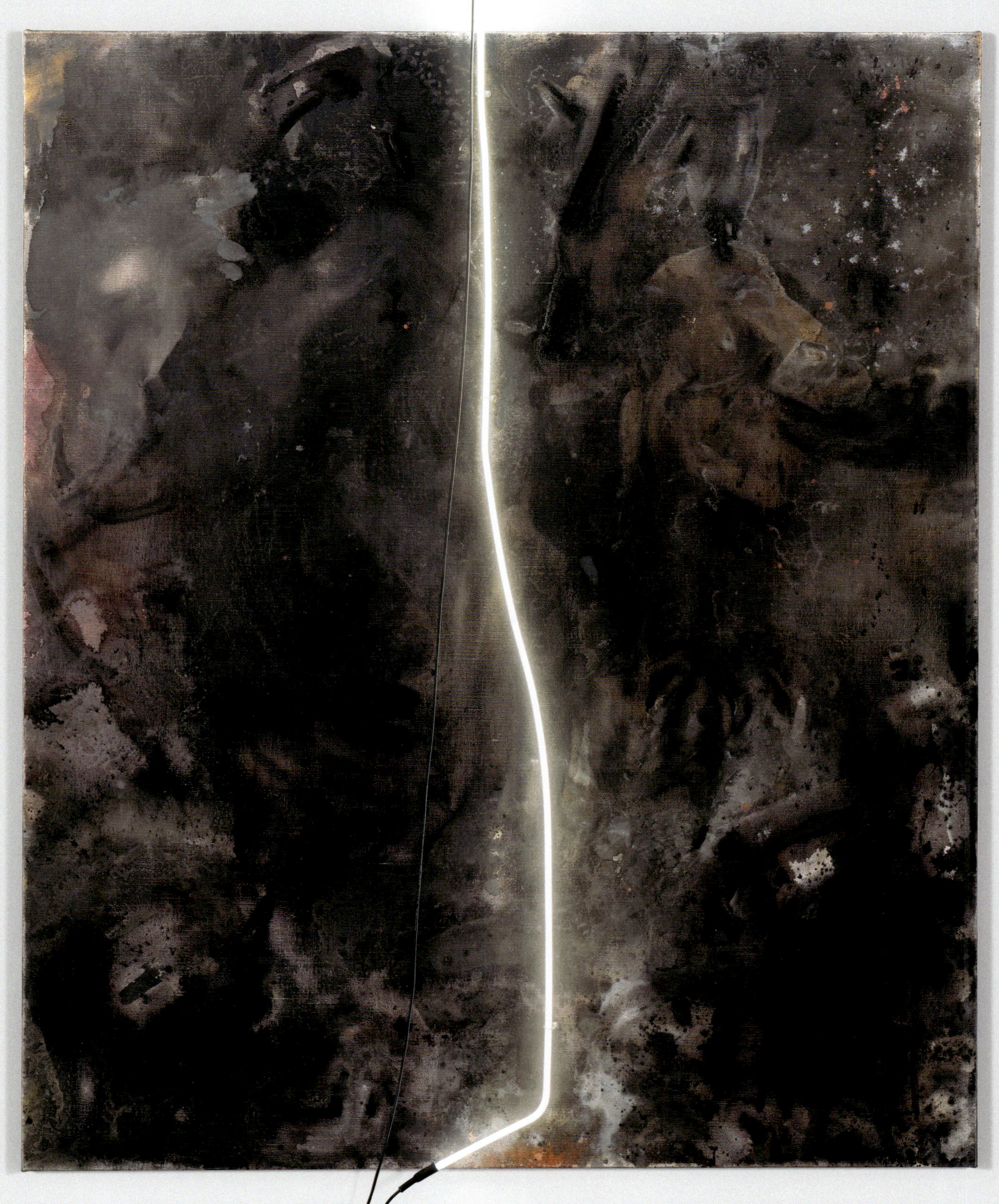

11 *The Flaying of Marsyas—5500 Spectra*, 2021–22

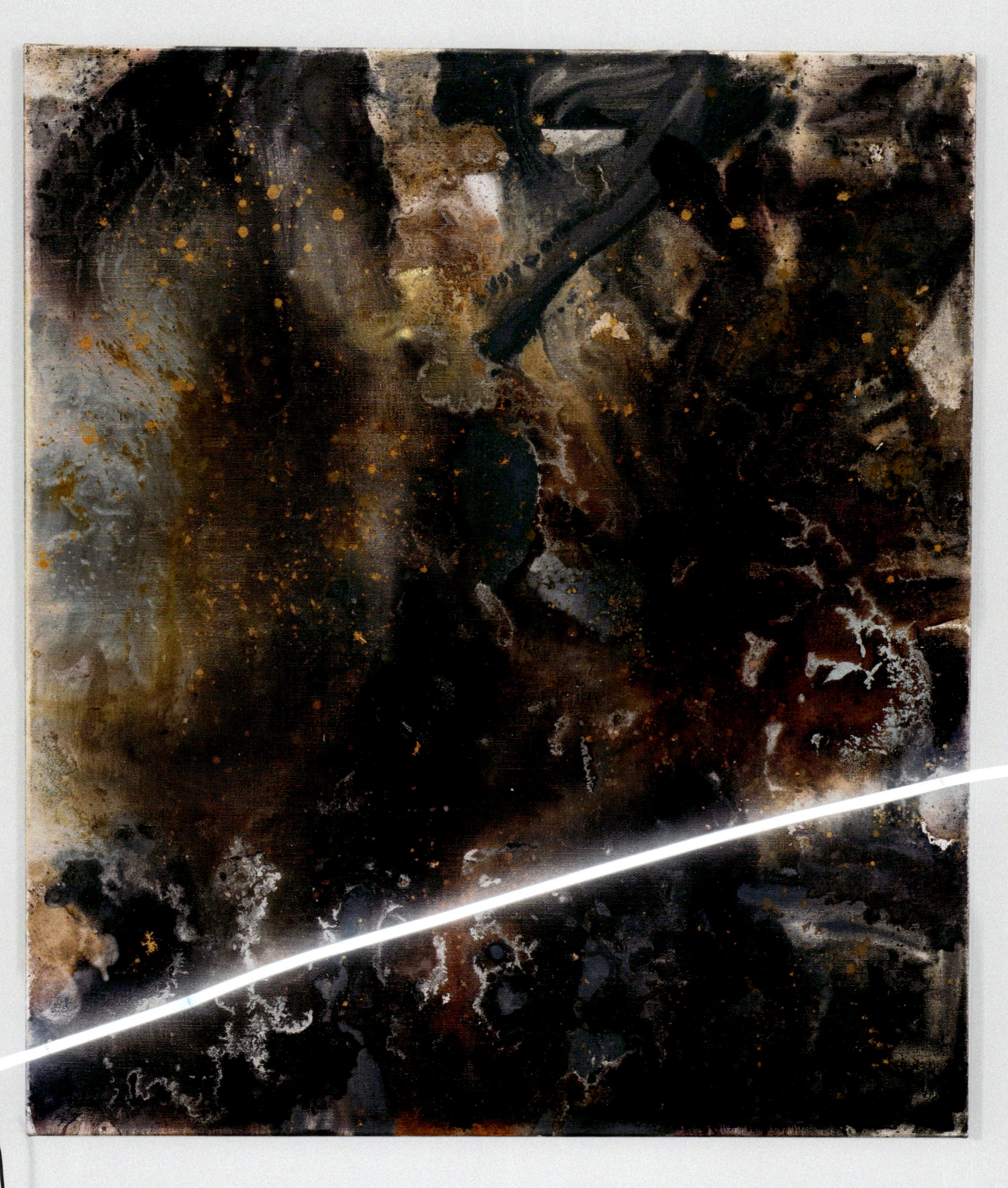

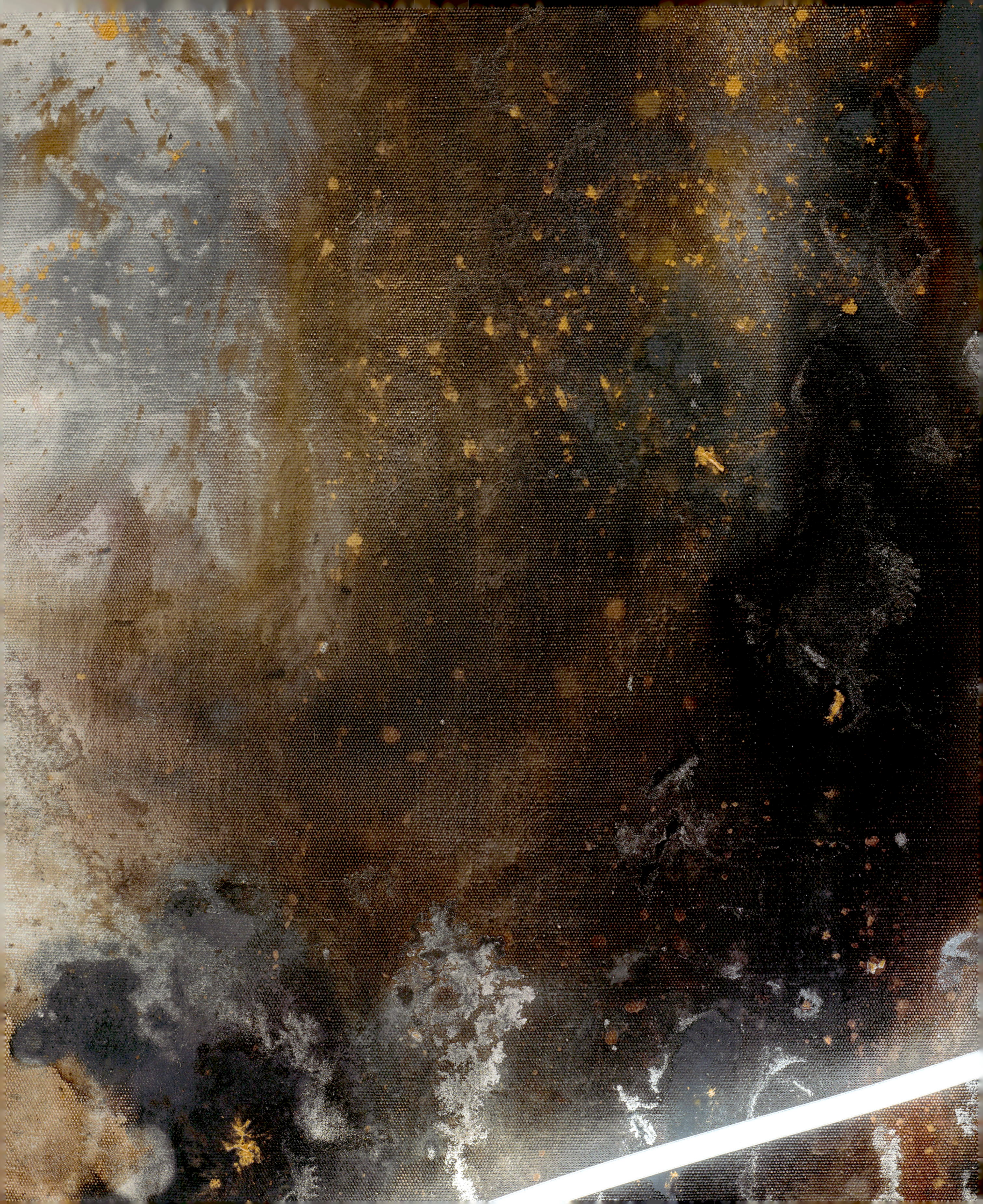

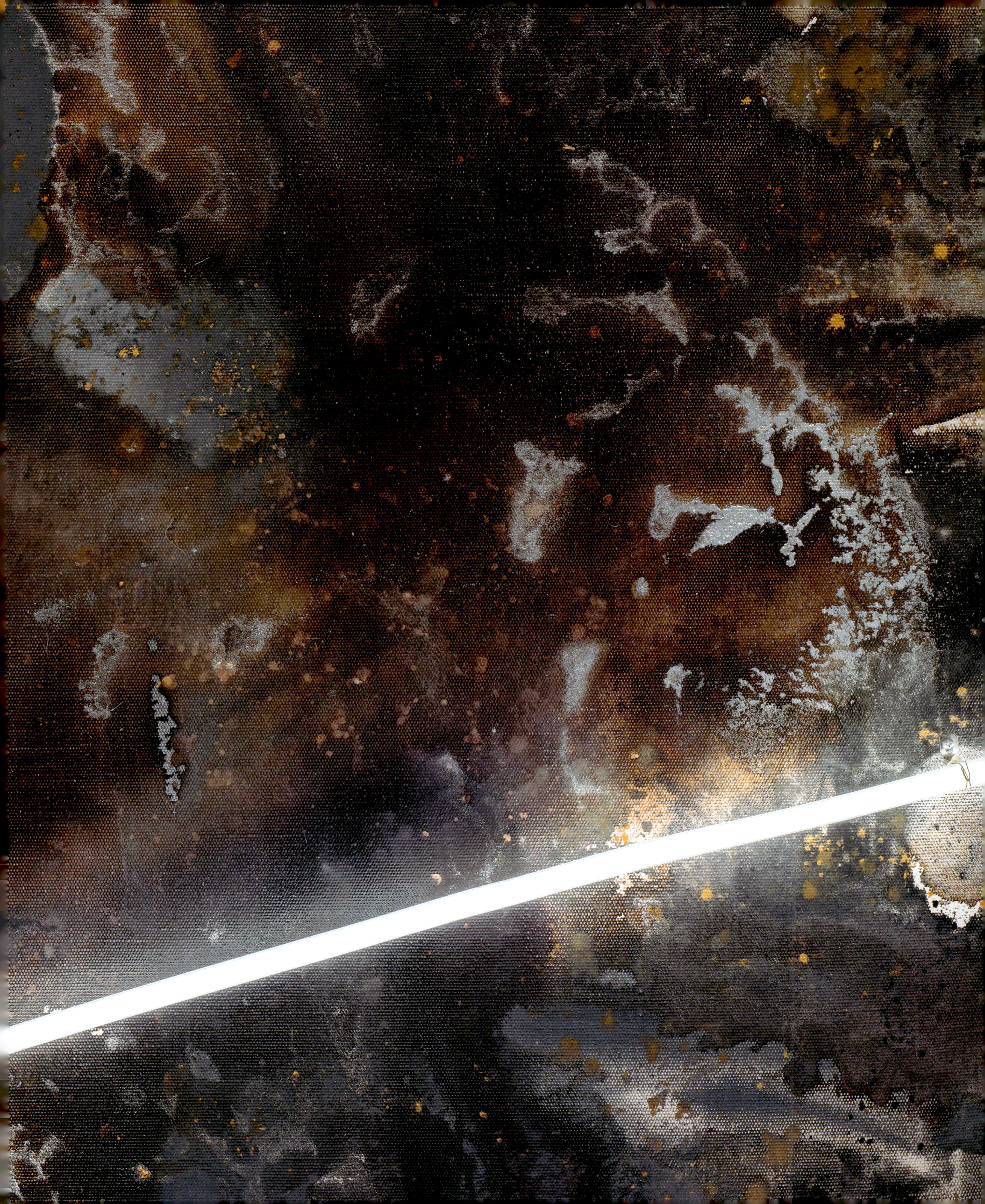

III *The Flaying of Marsyas—Warmtone*, 2021–22

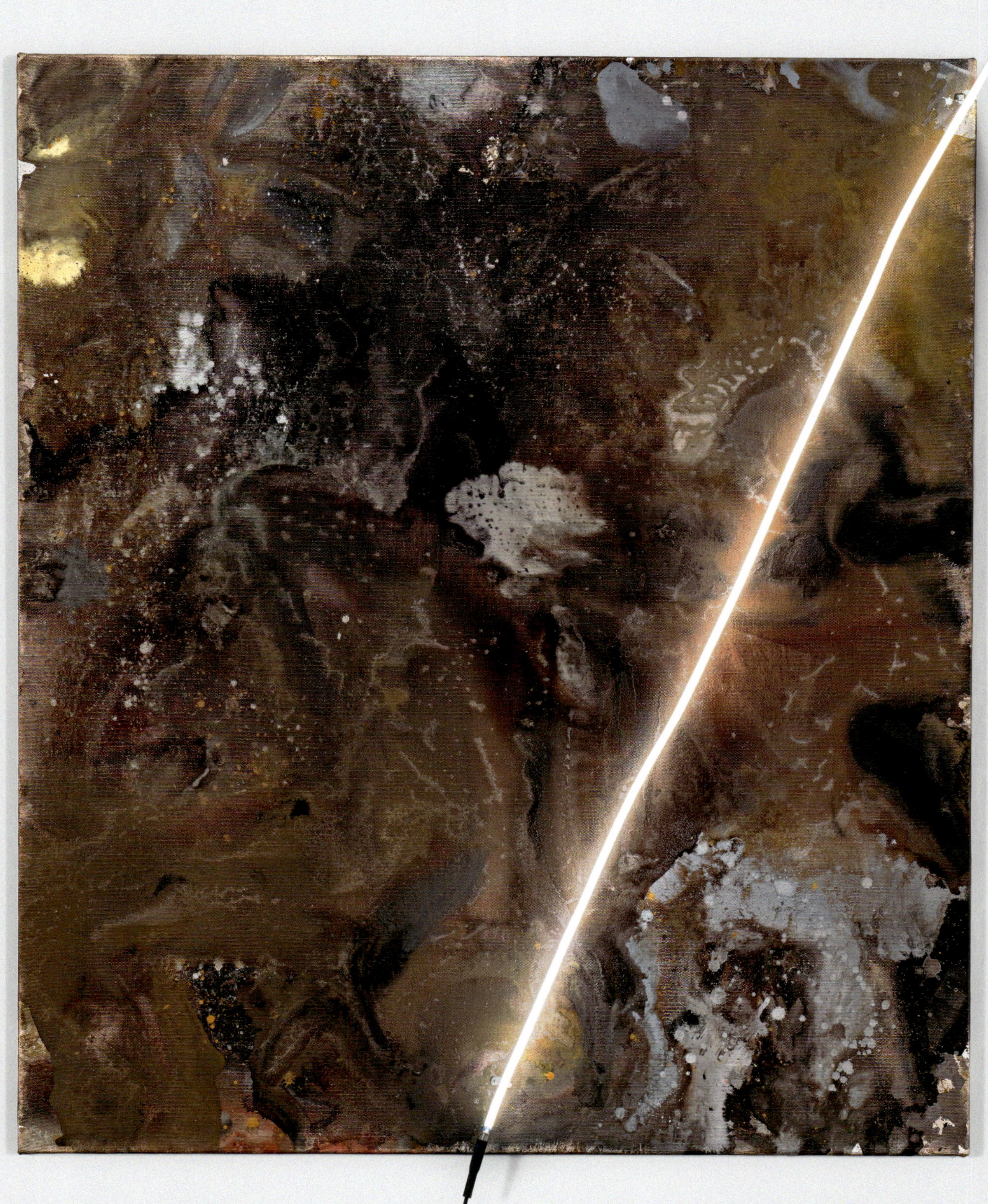

IV *The Flaying of Marsyas*, 2022

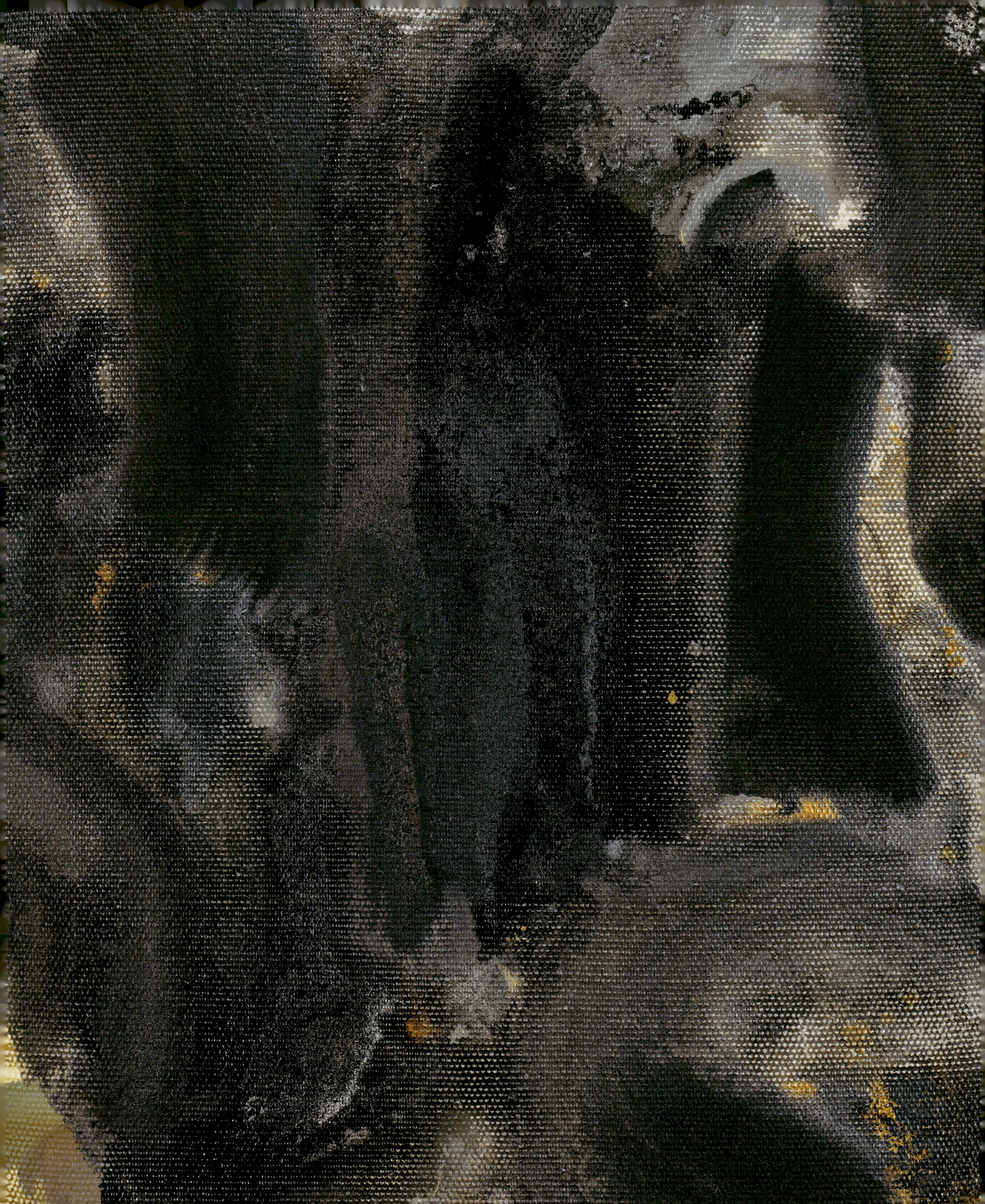

V *The Flaying of Marsyas—3500 Spectra*, 2021–22

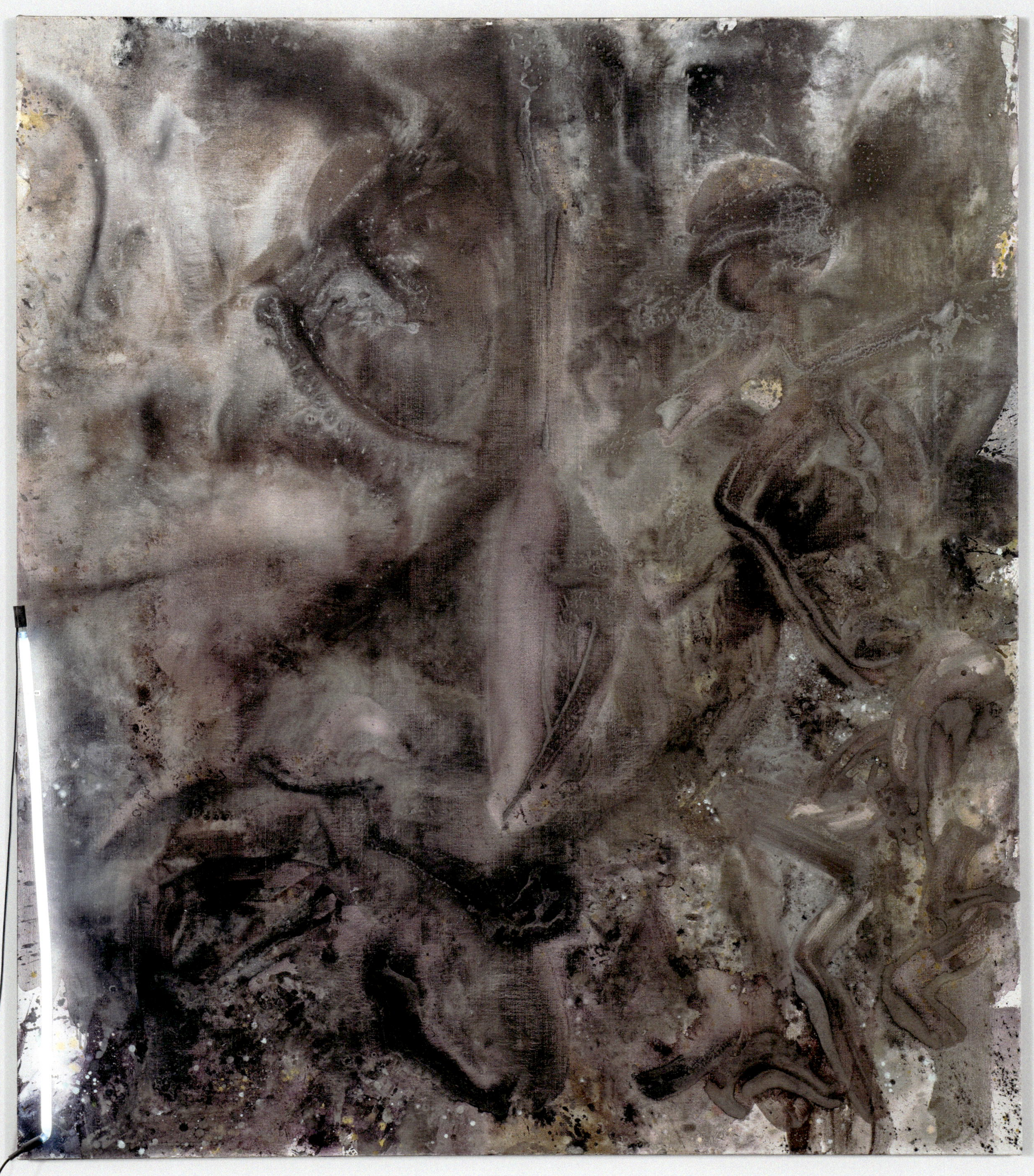

VI *The Flaying of Marsyas—Soft White and Sunrise*, 2021–22

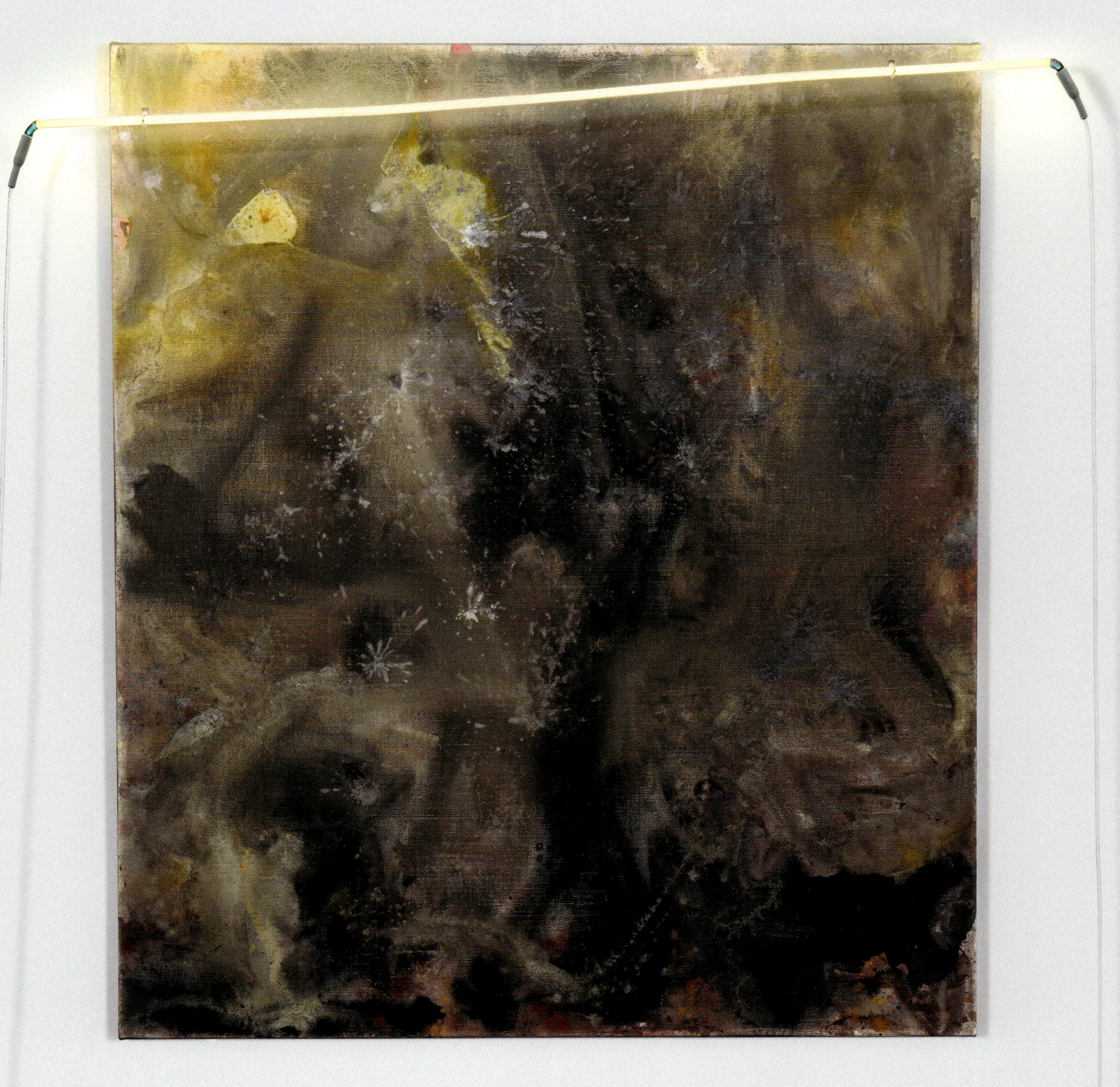

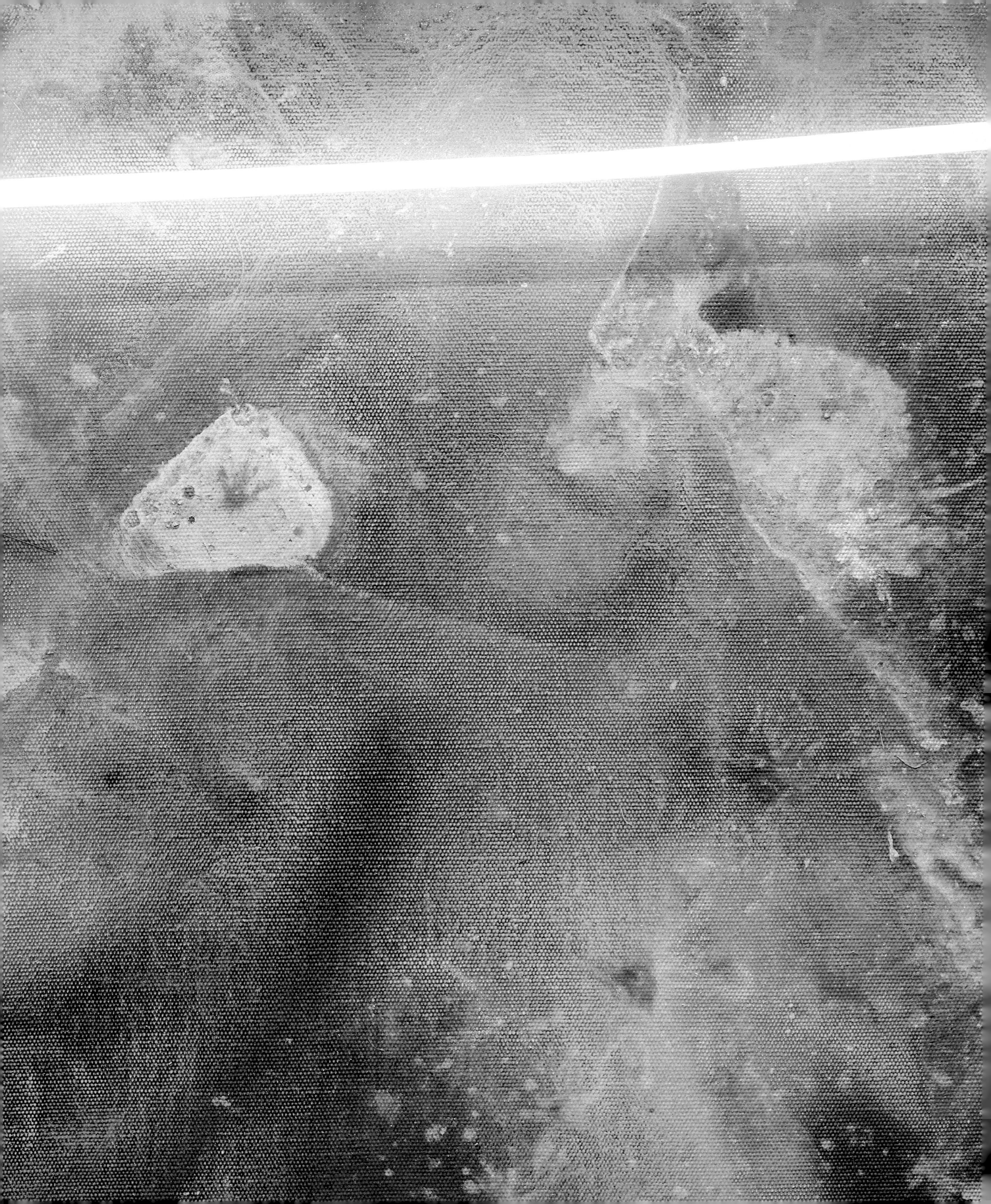

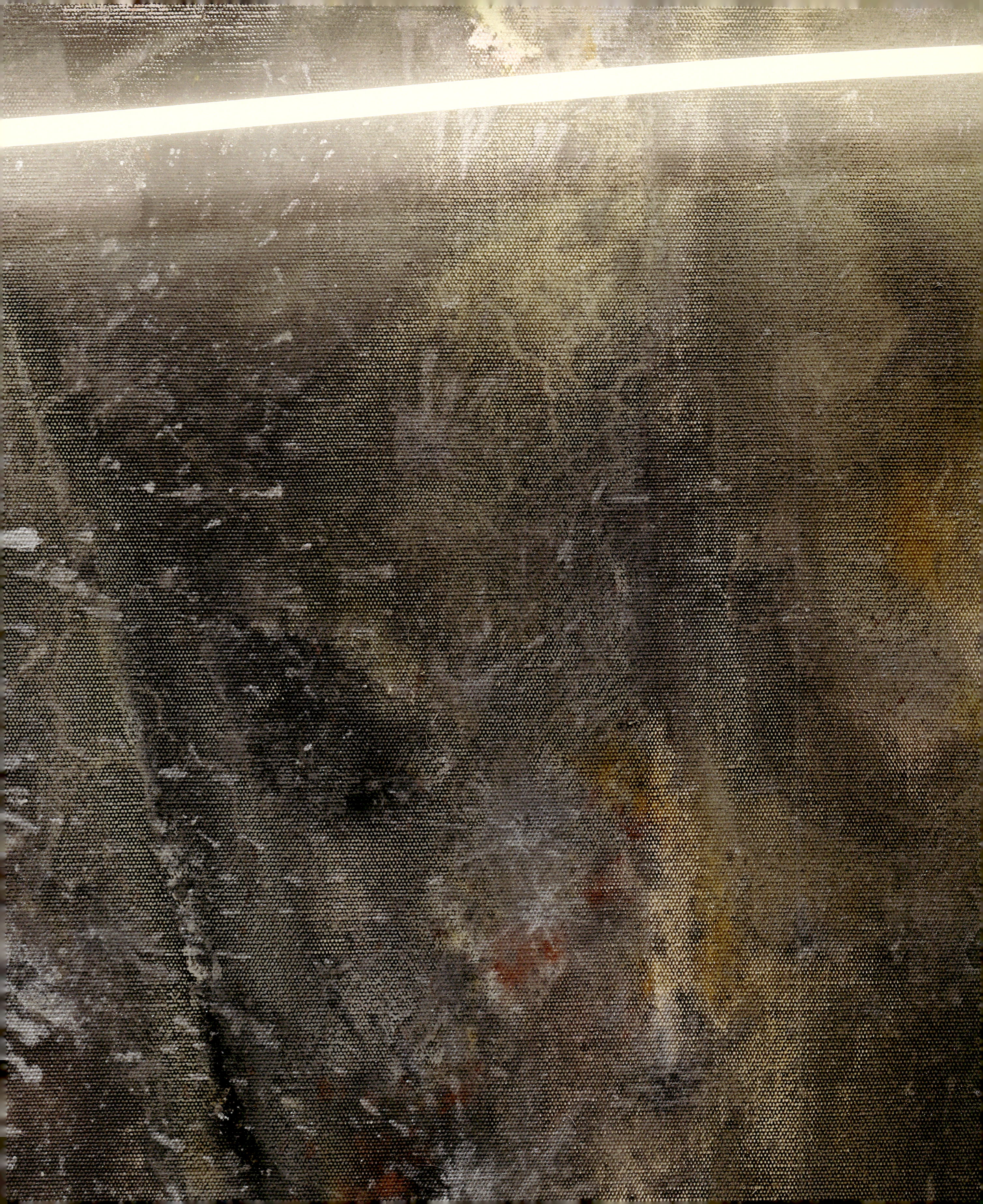

VII *The Flaying of Marsyas—4500 Triphosphor*, 2021–22

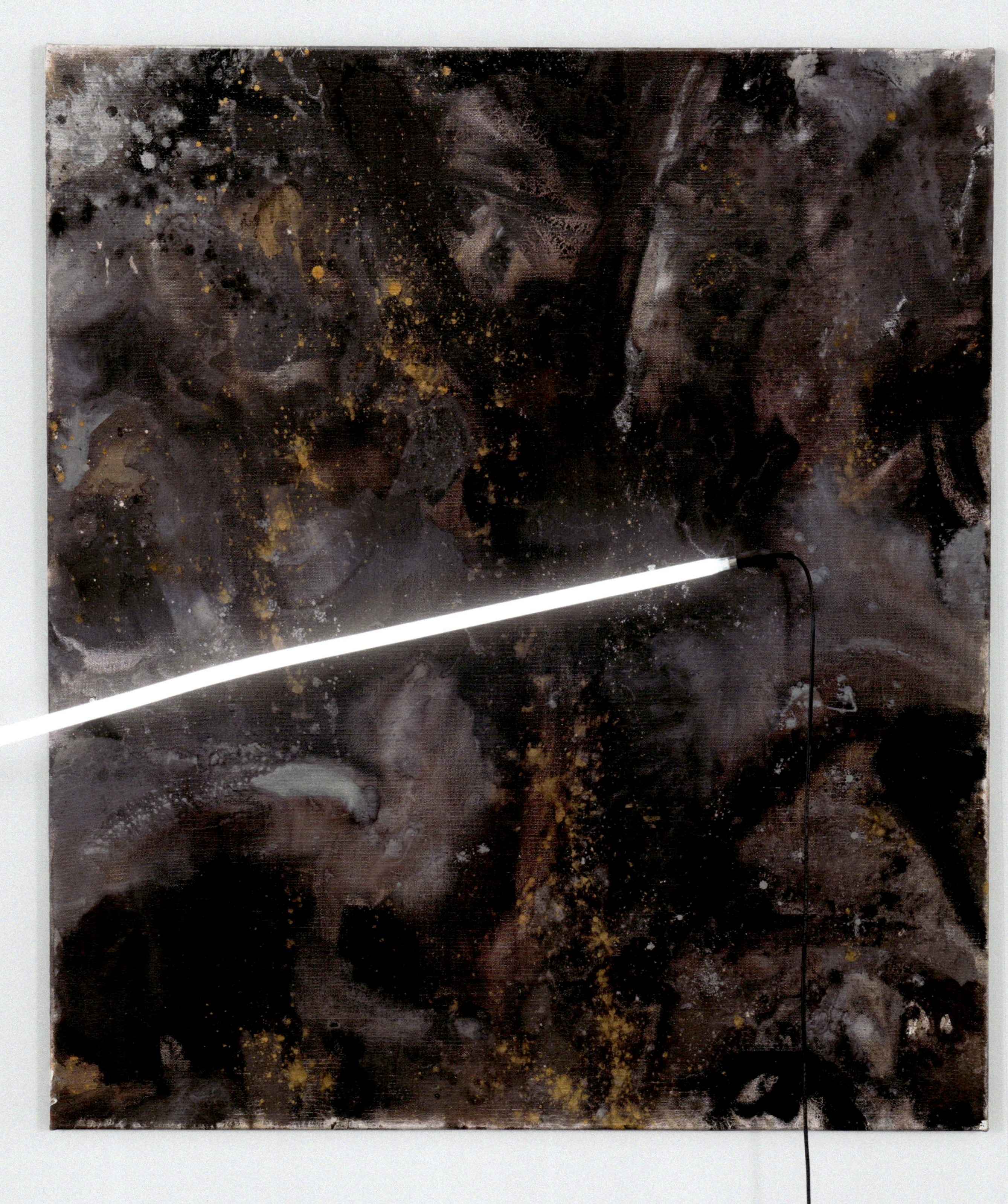

VIII *The Flaying of Marsyas—Satin and 4500 Triphosphor*, 2021–22

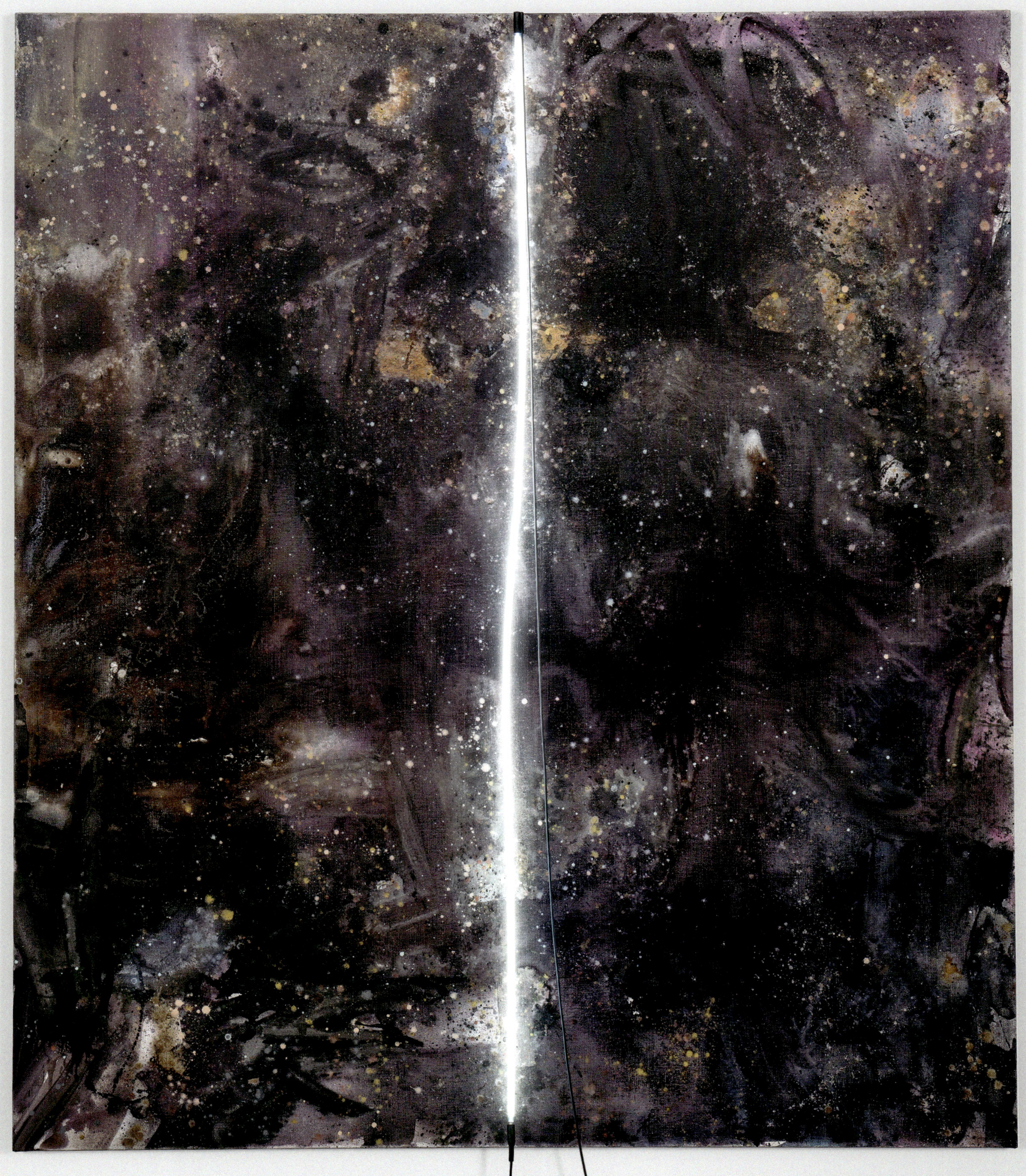

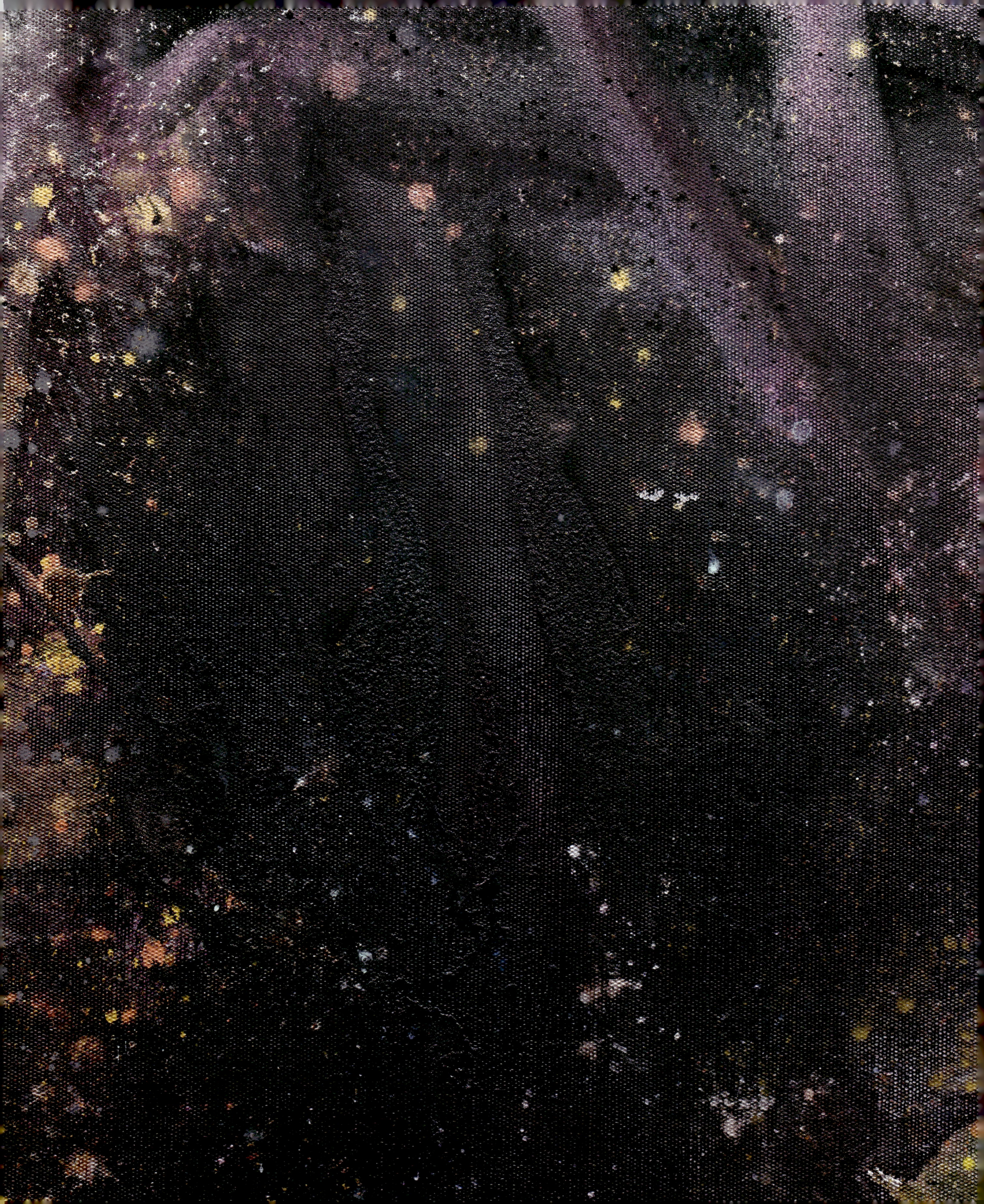

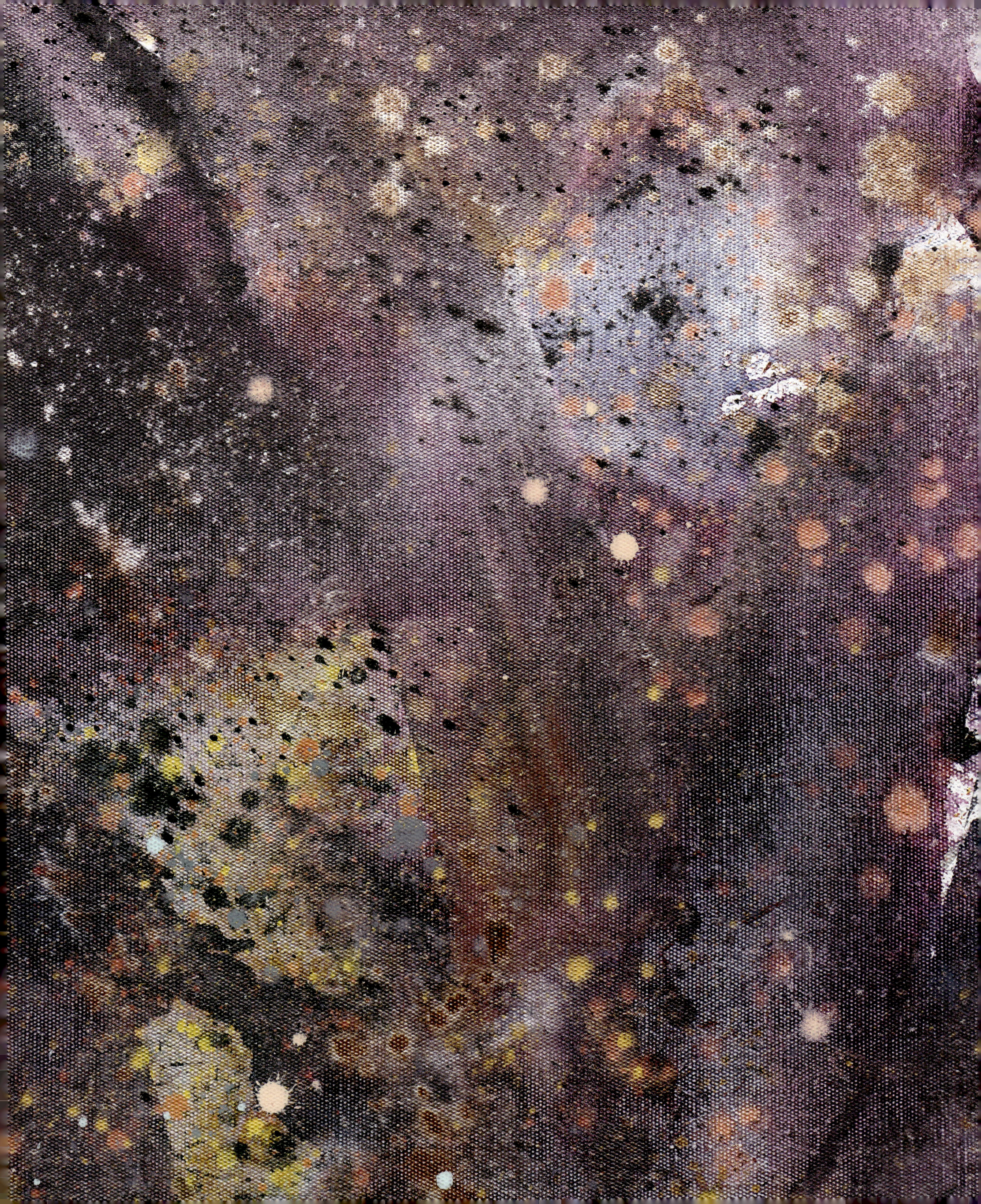

IX *The Flaying of Marsyas—Soft White*, 2021–22

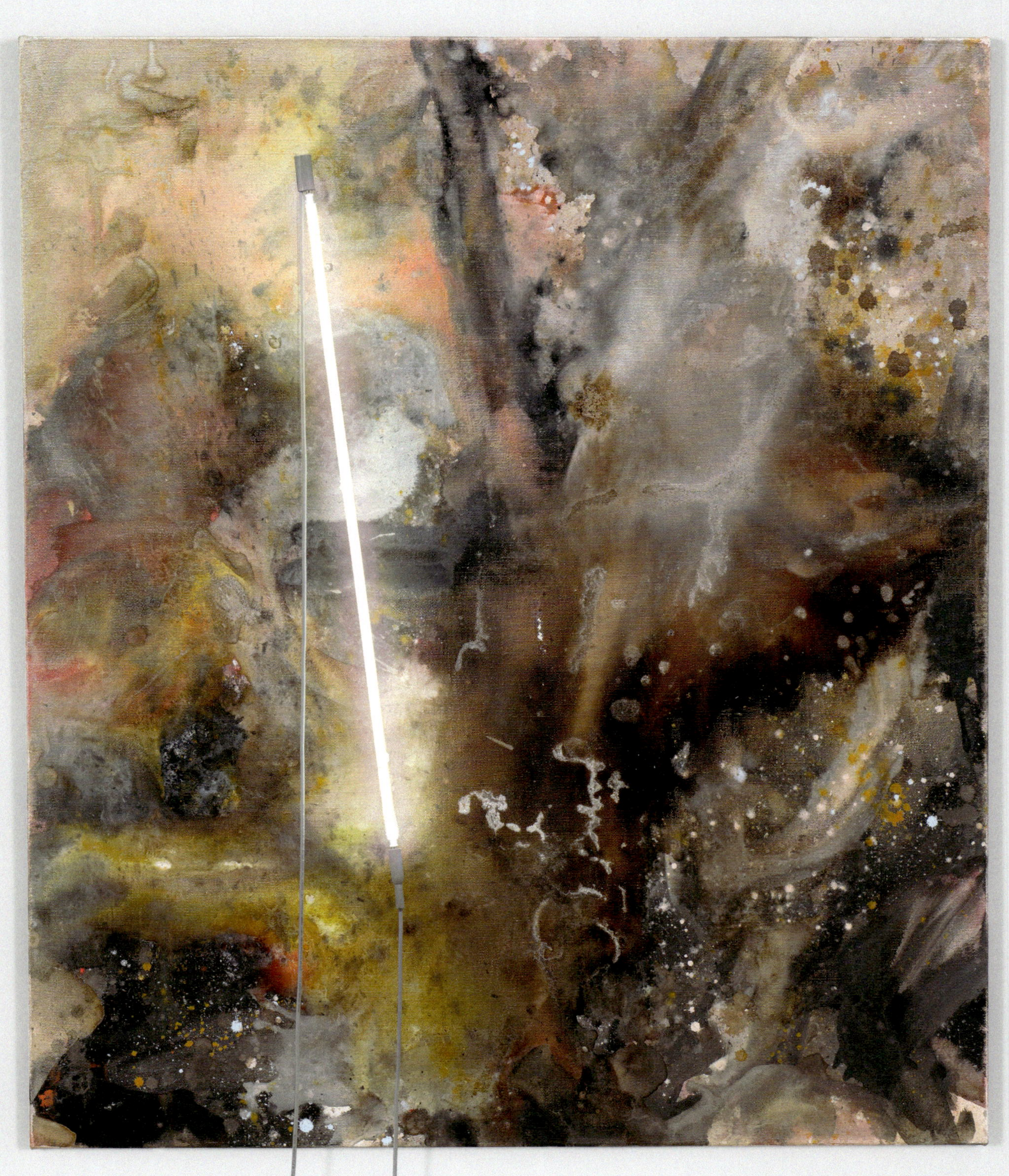

x *The Flaying of Marsyas—Sunrise and Soft White*, 2021–22

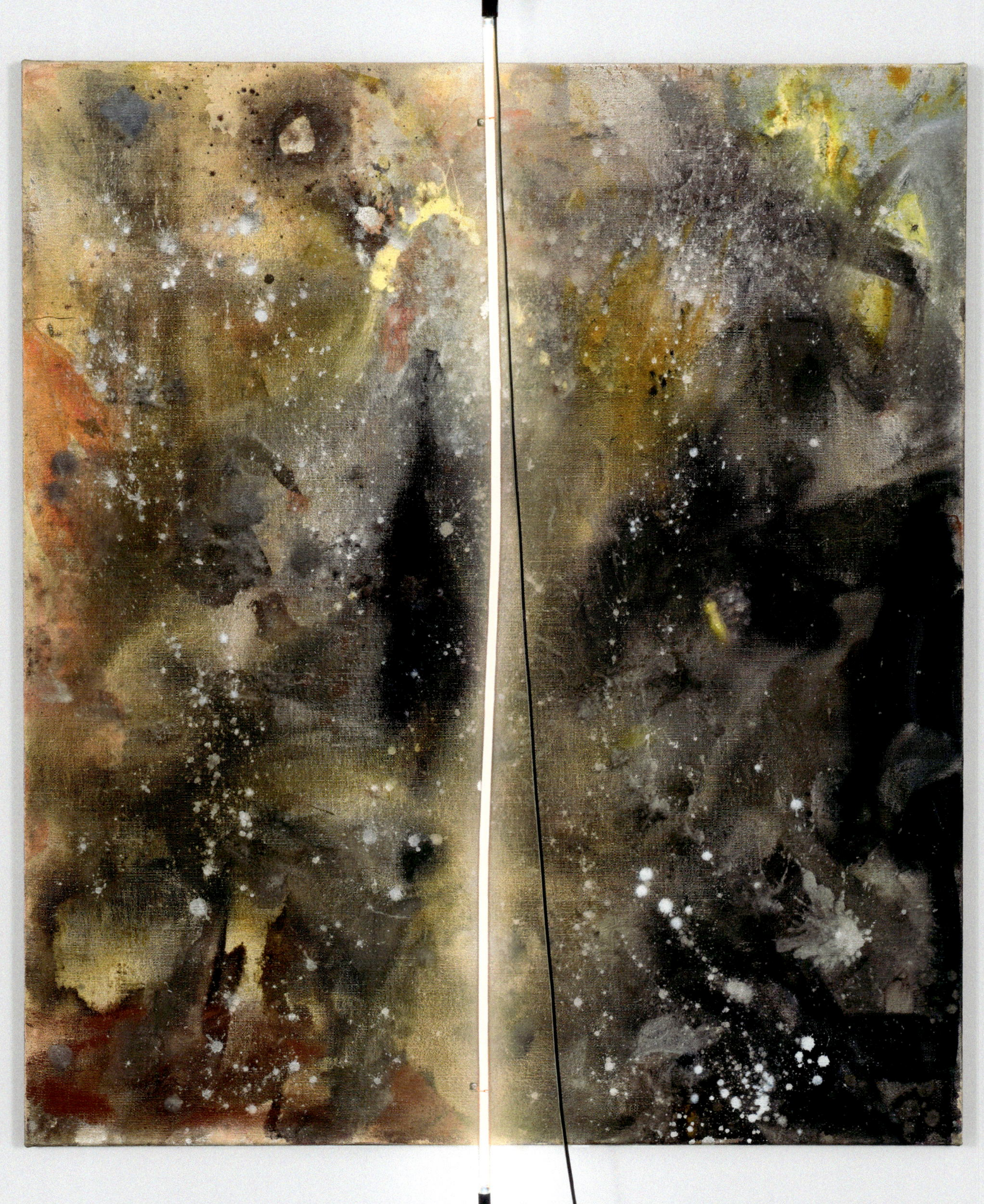

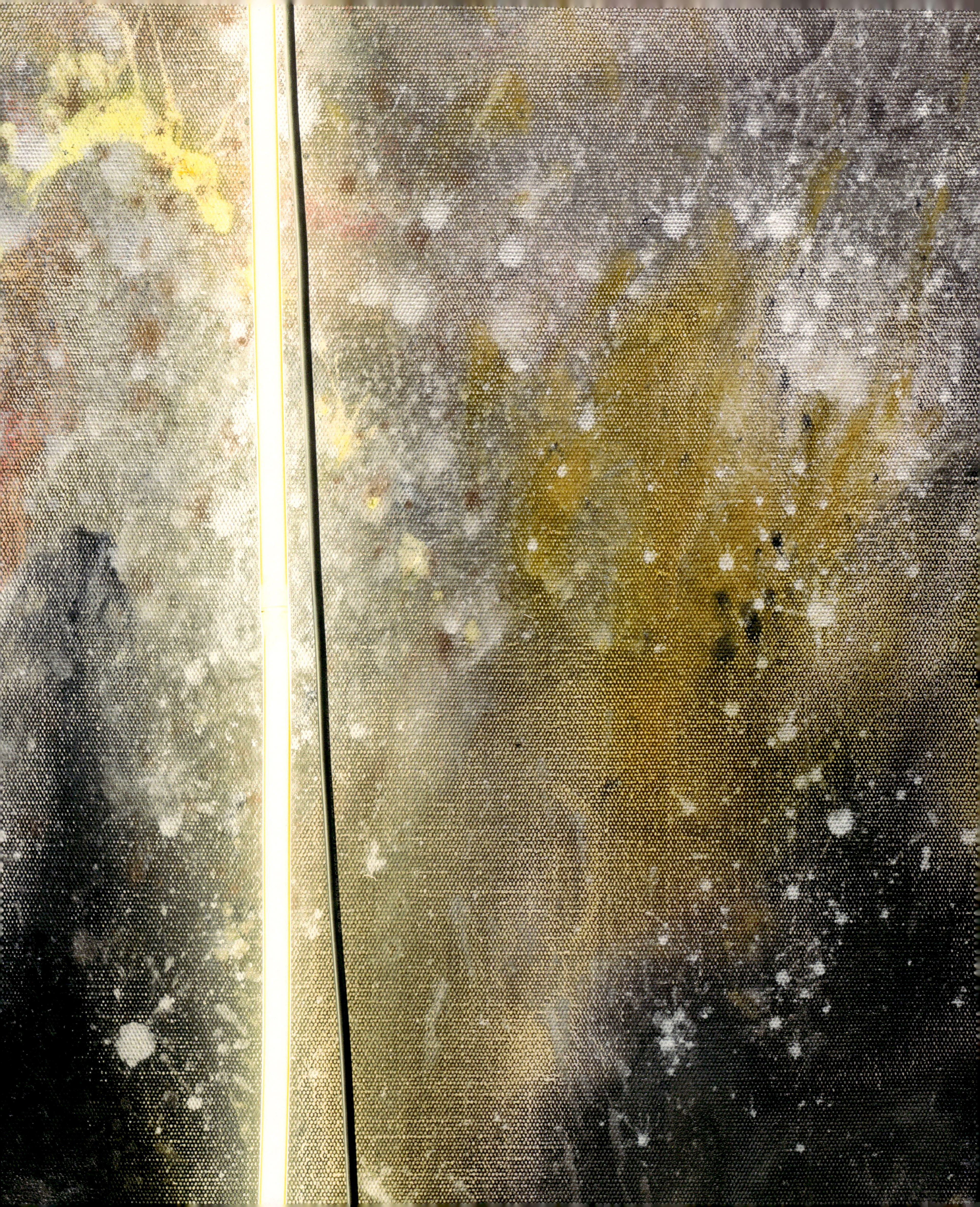

XI *The Flaying of Marsyas—Sunrise*, 2022

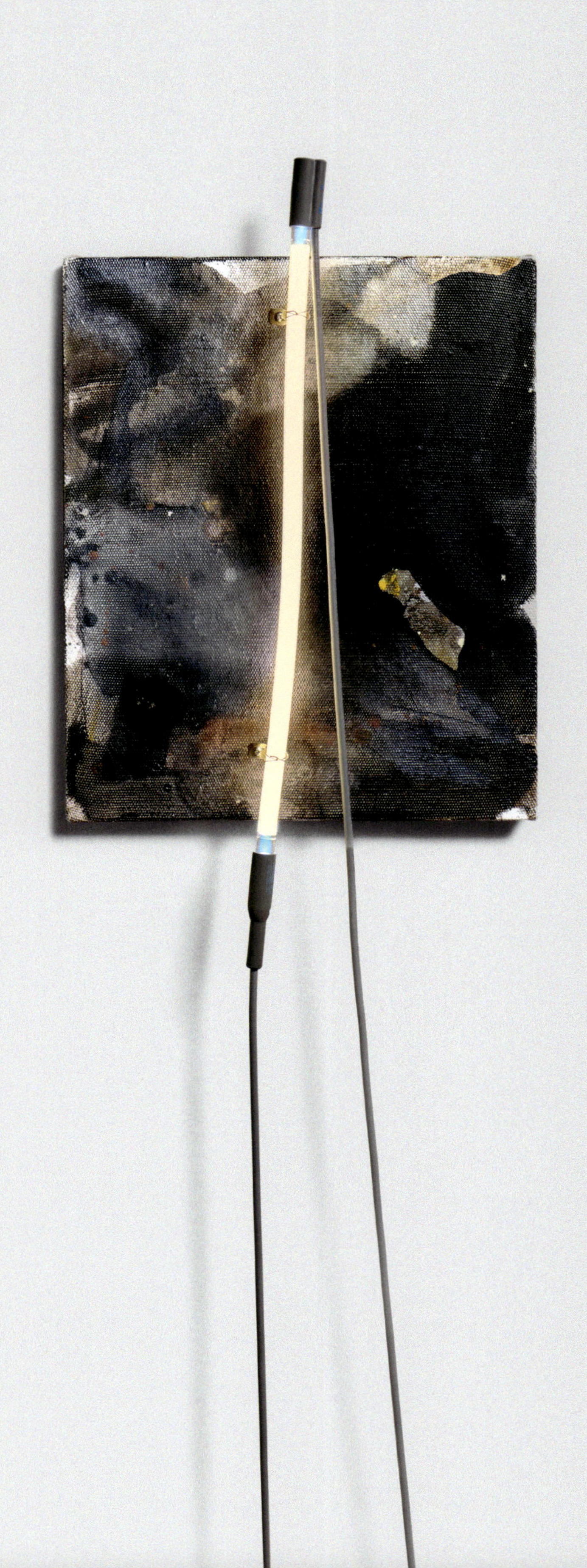

XII *The Flaying of Marsyas—Natural White and Satin*, 2021–22

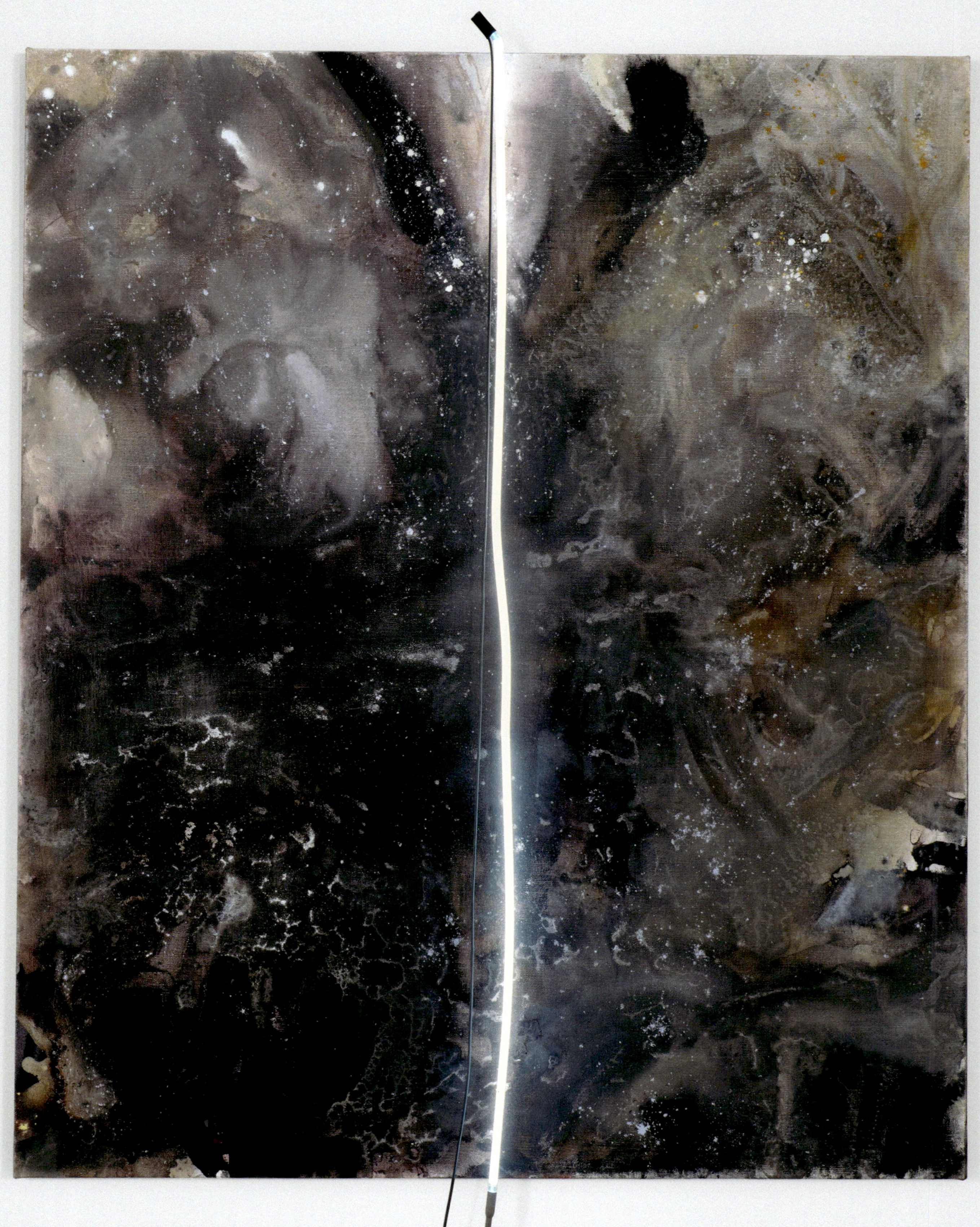

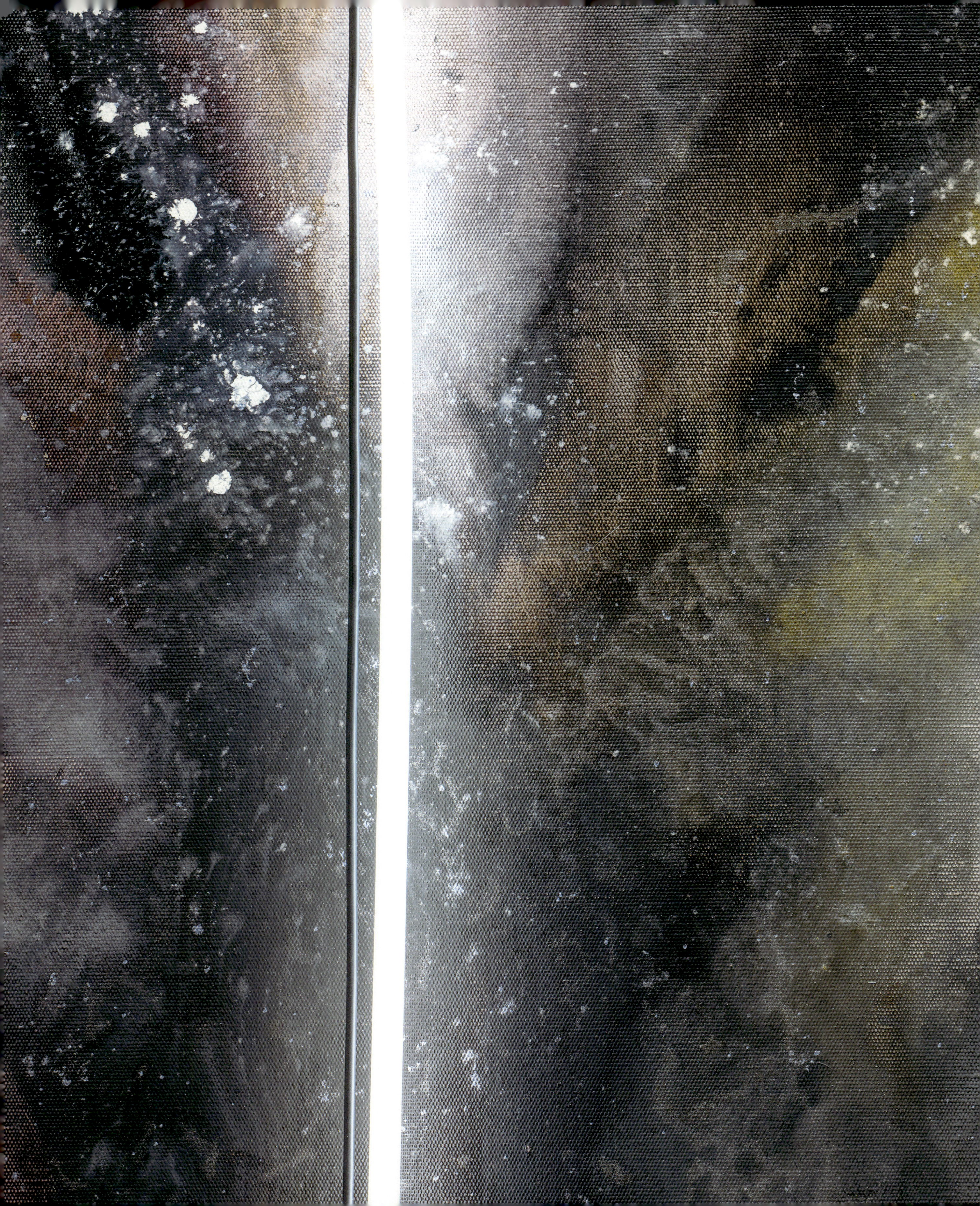

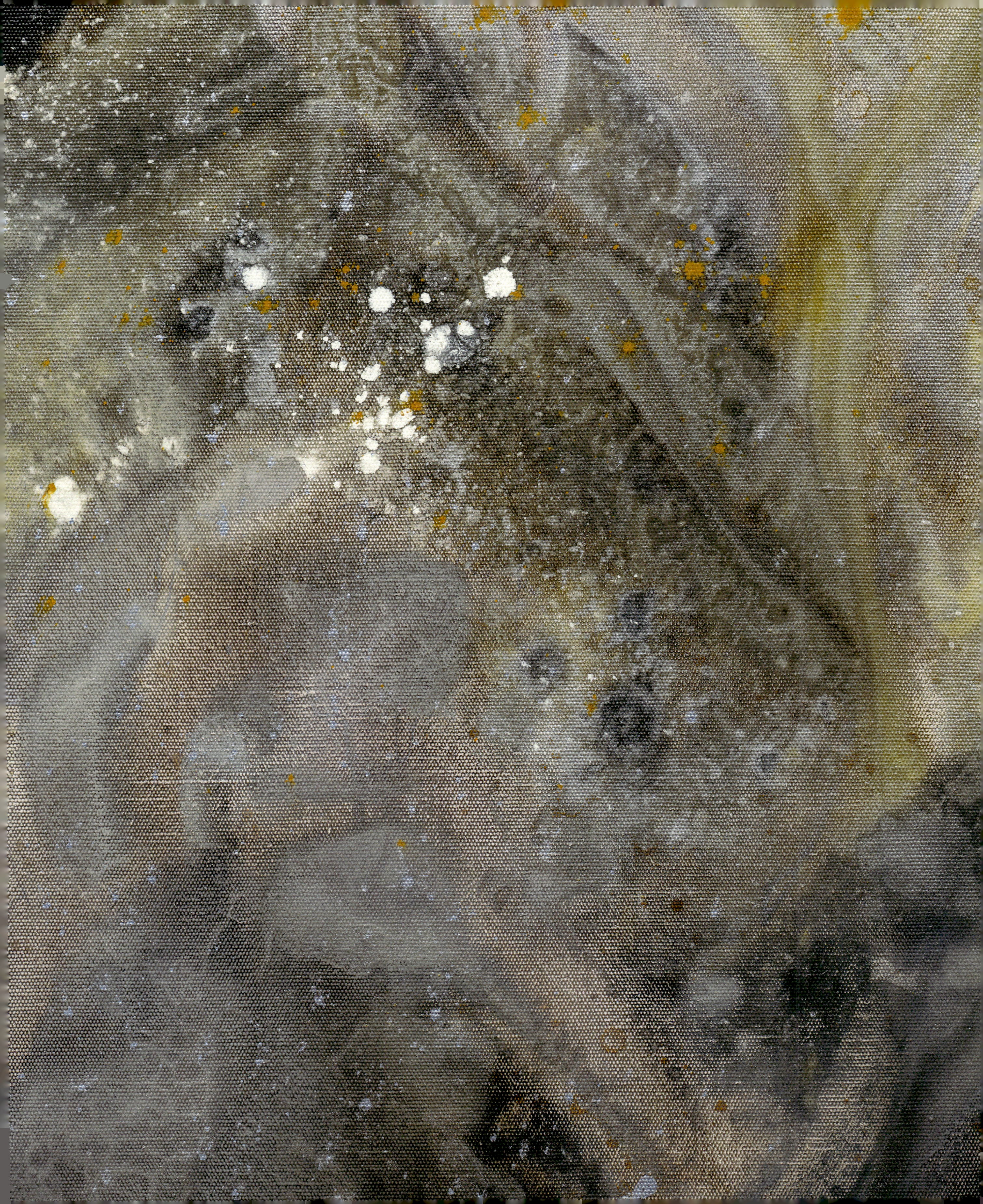

XIII *The Flaying of Marsyas—4100 Satin*, 2022

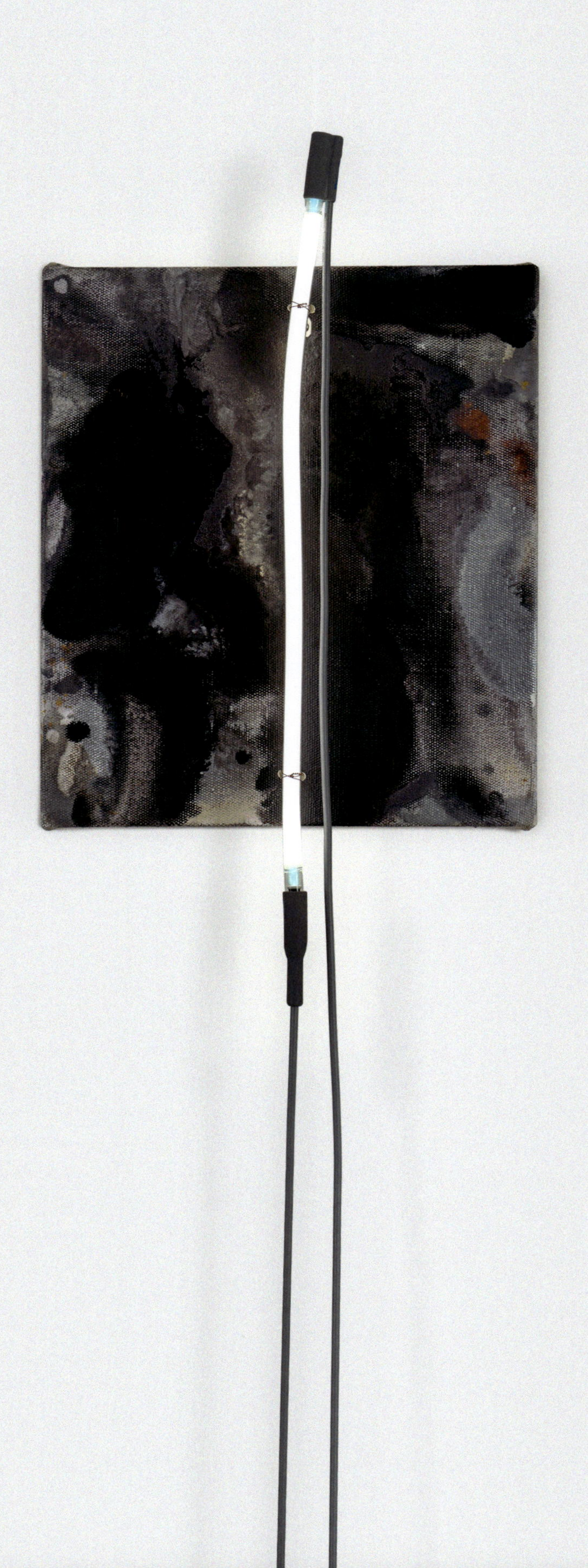

XIV *The Flaying of Marsyas—Natural White*, 2022

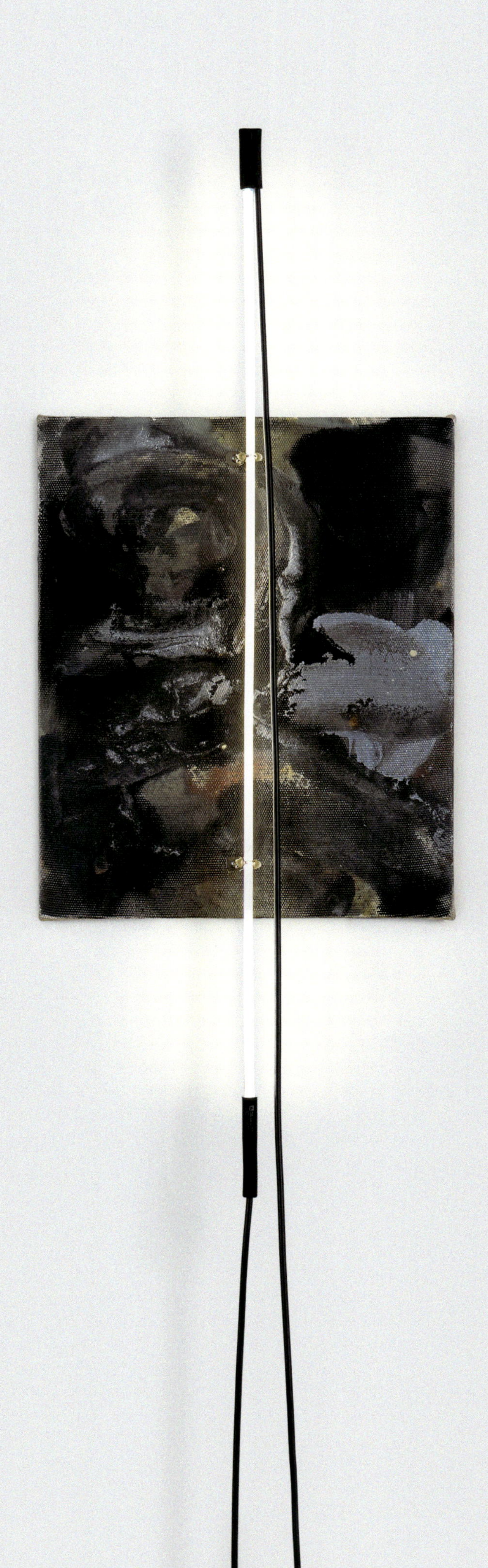

XV *The Flaying of Marsyas—Soft Triphosphor*, 2022

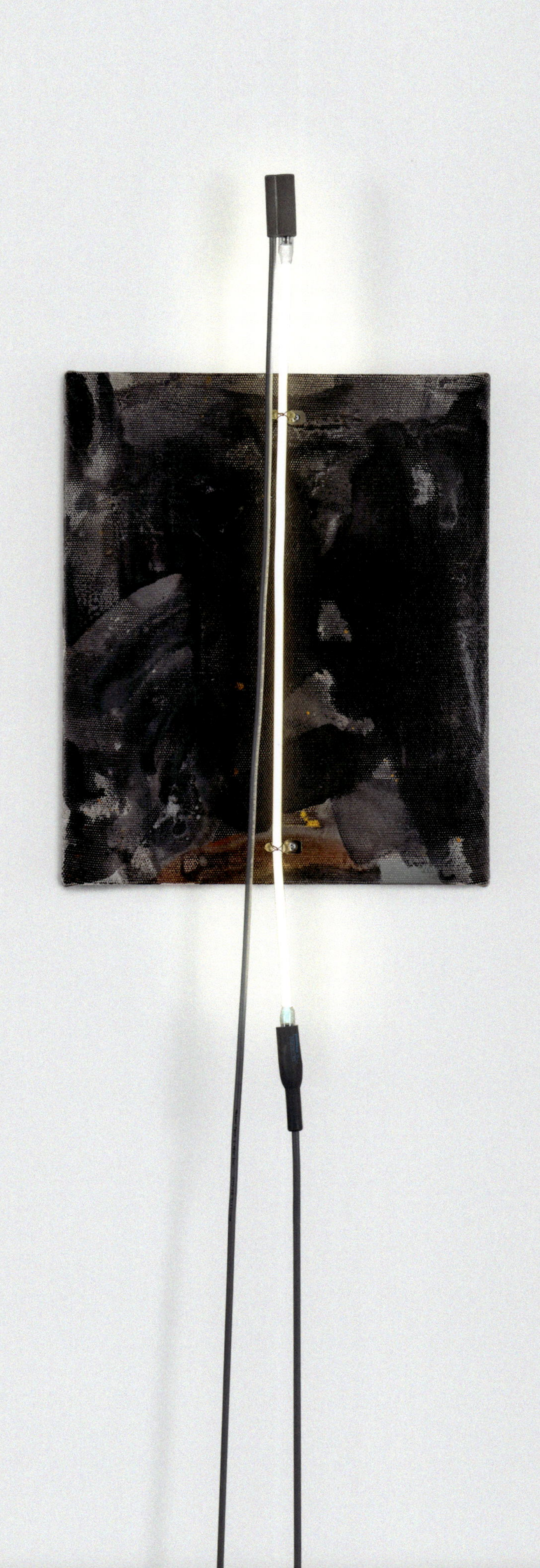

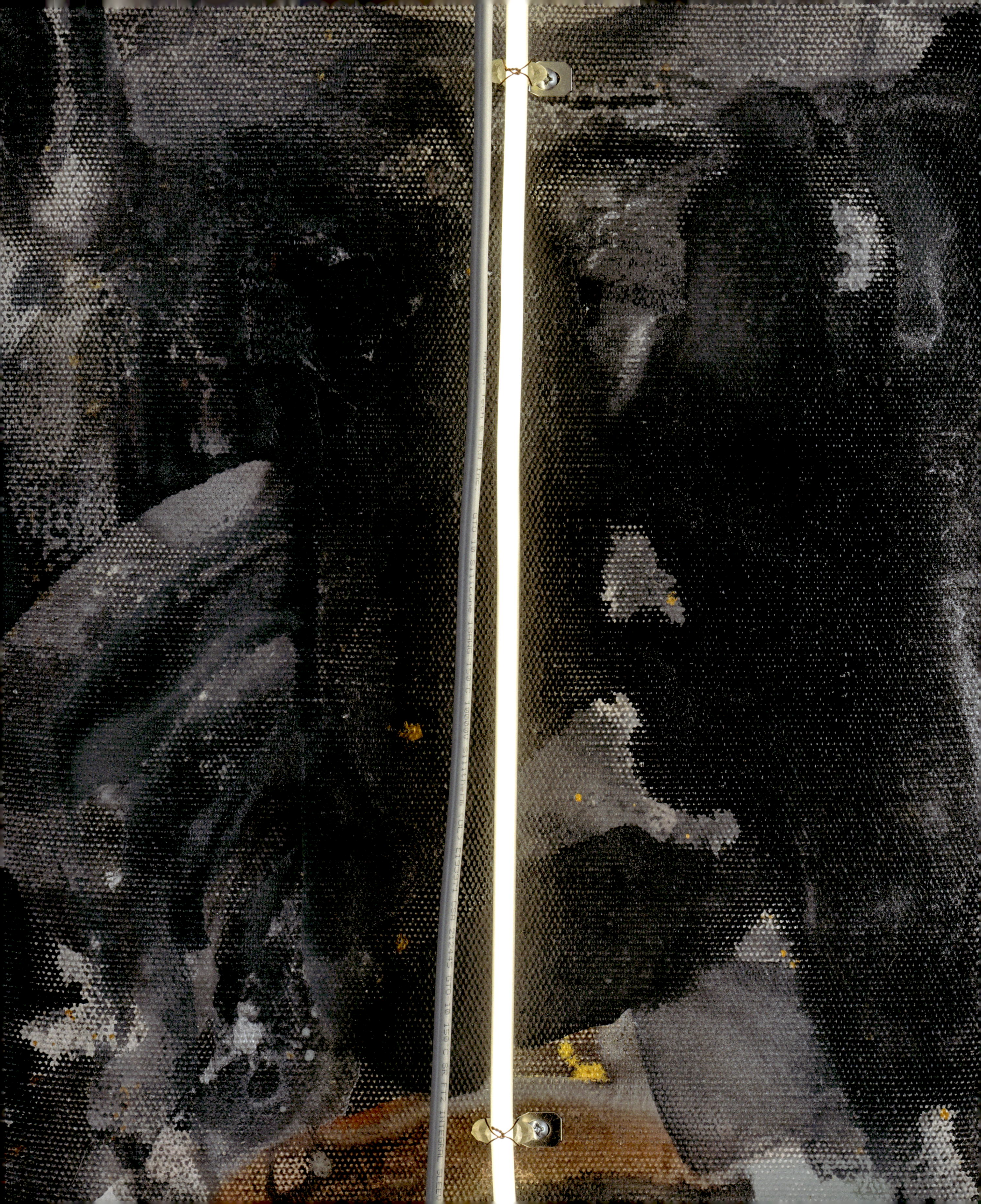

List of Works

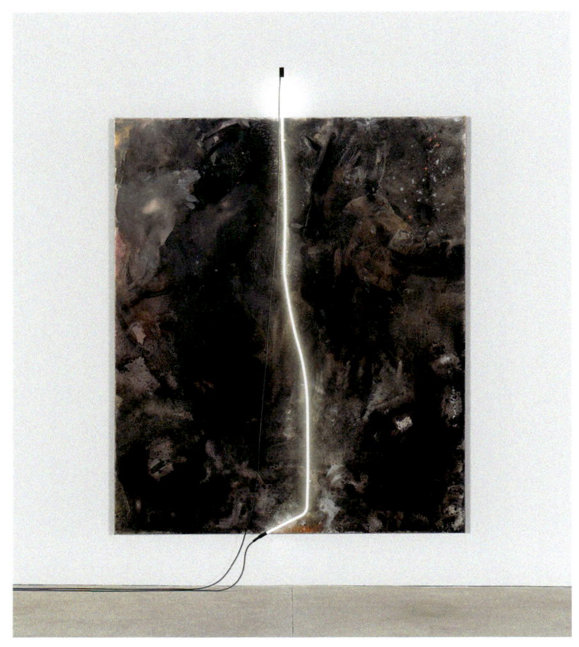

I
The Flaying of Marsyas—4500 Triphosphor, 2021–22
Flashe and neon on linen
93 × 79 inches (236.2 × 200.7 cm)

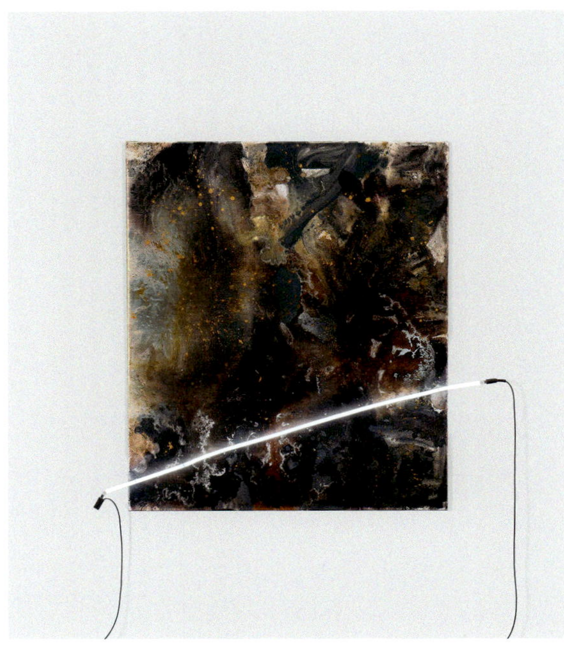

II
The Flaying of Marsyas—5500 Spectra, 2021–22
Flashe and neon on linen
66 × 58 inches (167.6 × 147.3 cm)

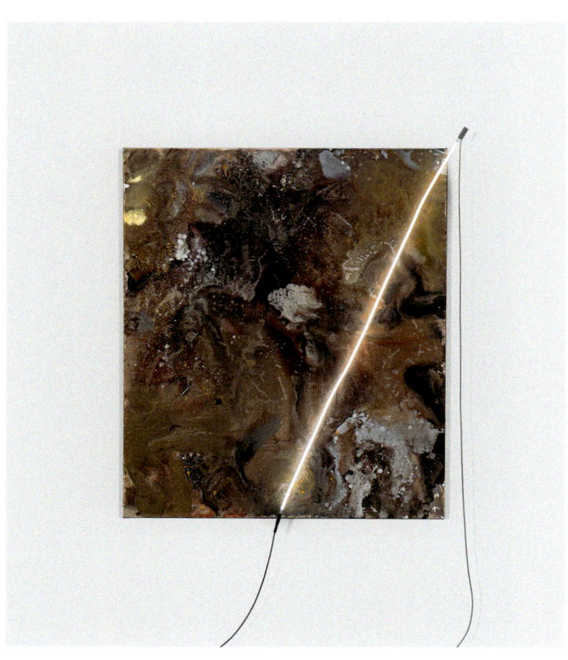

III
The Flaying of Marsyas—Warmtone, 2021–22
Flashe and neon on linen
66 × 58 inches (167.6 × 147.3 cm)

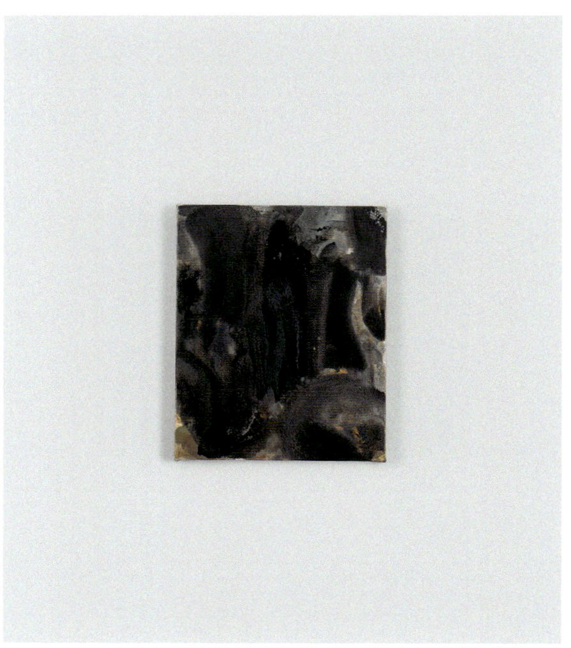

IV
The Flaying of Marsyas, 2022
Flashe on linen
18 × 15 inches (45.7 × 38.1 cm)

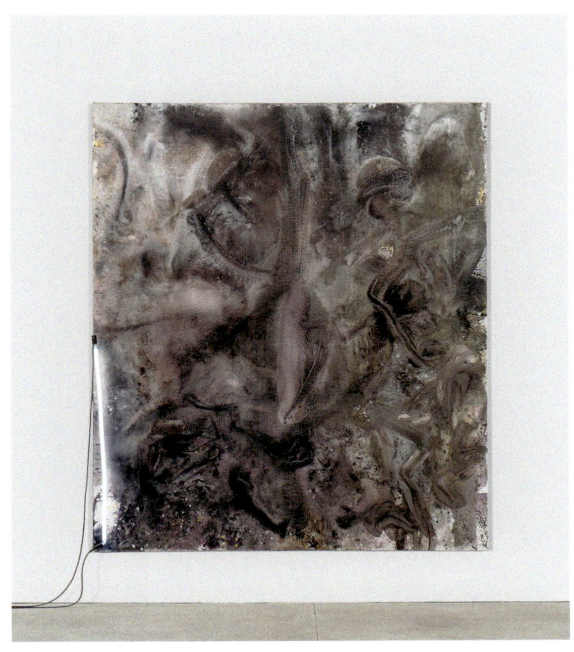

V
The Flaying of Marsyas—3500 Spectra, 2021–22
Flashe and neon on linen
112 × 99 inches (284.5 × 251.5 cm)

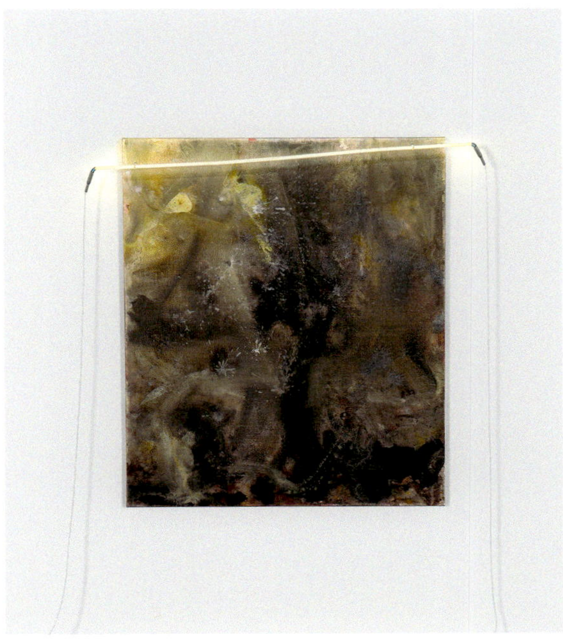

VI
The Flaying of Marsyas—Soft White and Sunrise, 2021–22
Flashe and neon on linen
66 × 58 inches (167.6 × 147.3 cm)

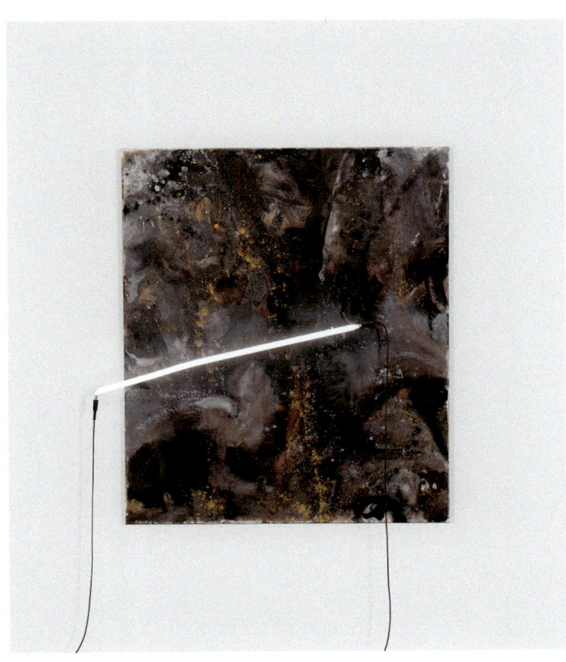

VII
The Flaying of Marsyas—4500 Triphosphor, 2021–22
Flashe and neon on linen
66 × 58 inches (167.6 × 147.3 cm)

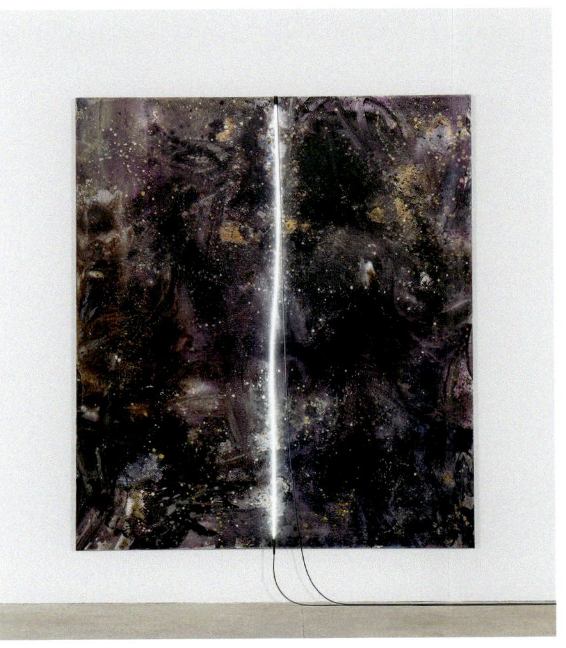

VIII
The Flaying of Marsyas—Satin and 4500 Triphosphor, 2021–22
Flashe and neon on linen
112 × 99 inches (284.5 × 251.5 cm)

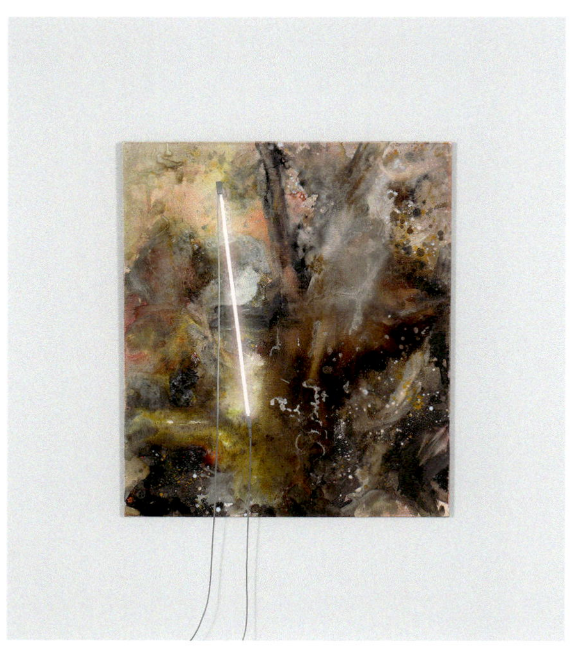

IX
The Flaying of Marsyas—Soft White, 2021–22
Flashe and neon on linen
66 × 58 inches (167.6 × 147.3 cm)

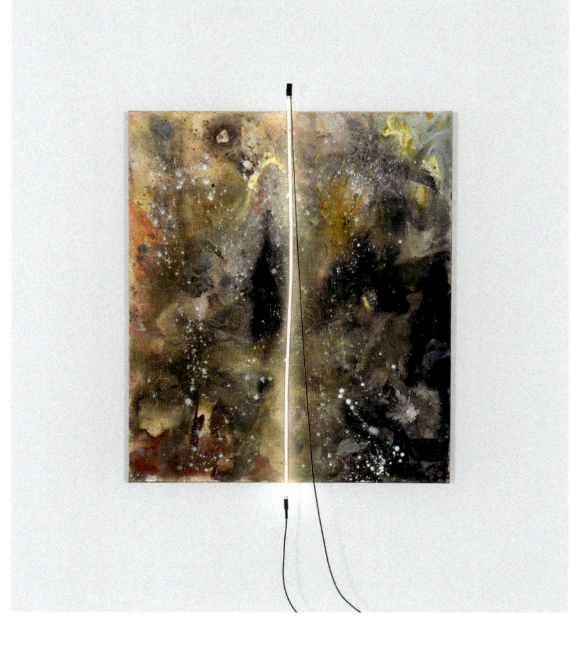

X
The Flaying of Marsyas—Sunrise and Soft White, 2021–22
Flashe and neon on linen
66 × 58 inches (167.6 × 147.3 cm)

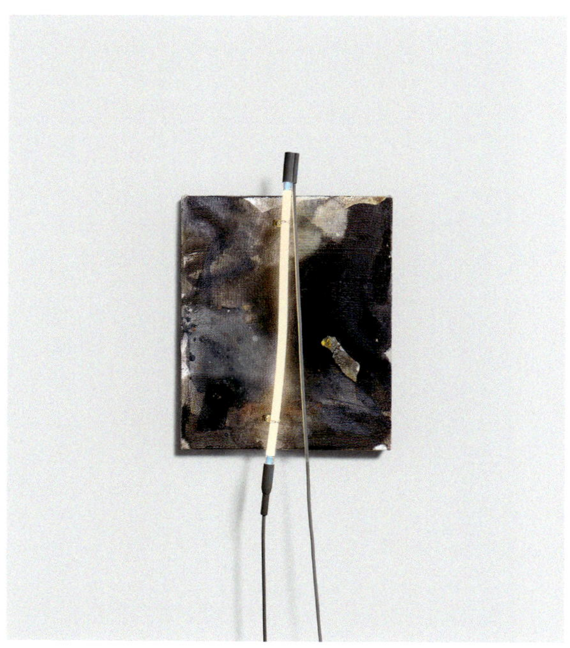

XI
The Flaying of Marsyas—Sunrise, 2022
Flashe and neon on linen
18 × 15 inches (45.7 × 38.1 cm)

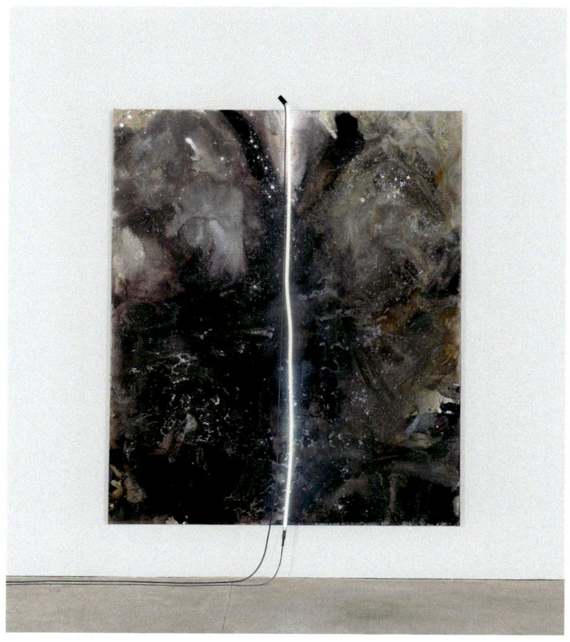

XII
The Flaying of Marsyas—Natural White and Satin, 2021–22
Flashe and neon on linen
93 × 79 inches (236.2 × 200.7 cm)

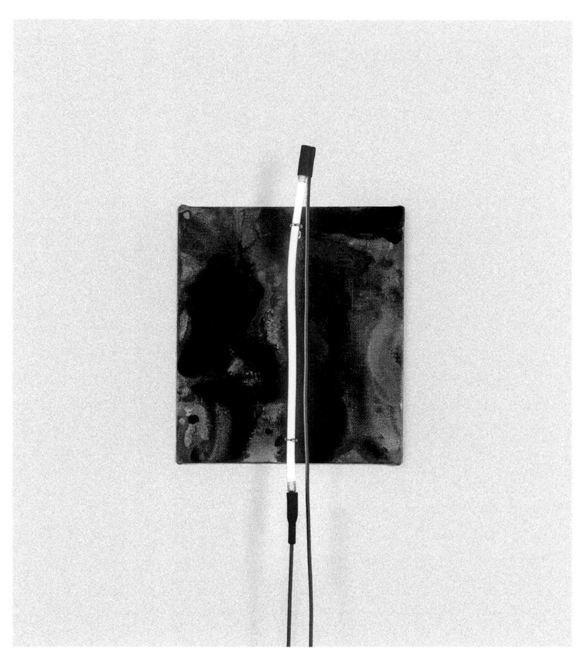

XIII
The Flaying of Marsyas—4100 Satin, 2022*
Flashe and neon on linen
18 × 16 inches (45.7 × 40.6 cm)

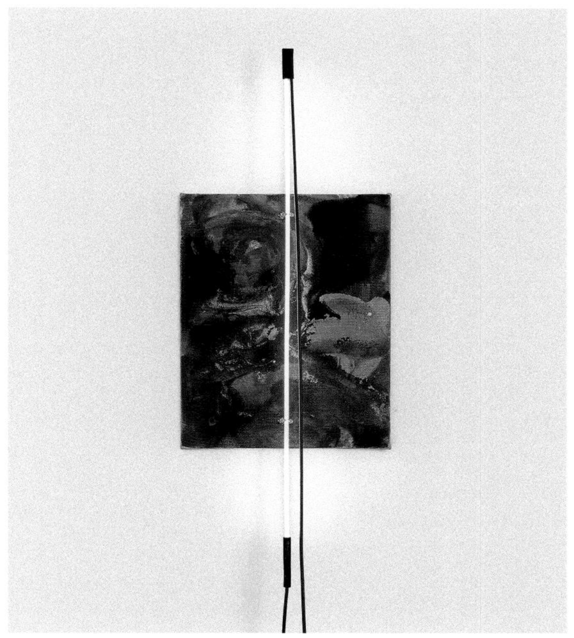

XIV
The Flaying of Marsyas—Natural White, 2022*
Flashe and neon on linen
18 × 15 inches (45.7 × 38.1 cm)

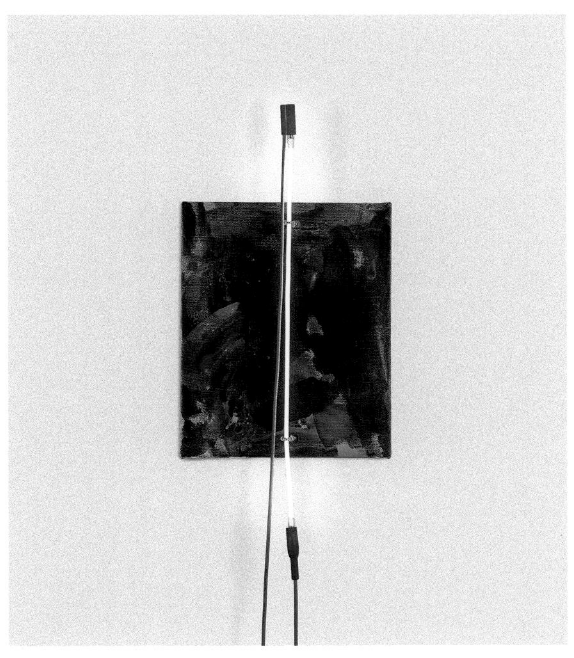

XV
The Flaying of Marsyas—Soft Triphosphor, 2022*
Flashe and neon on linen
18 × 15 inches (45.7 × 38.1 cm)

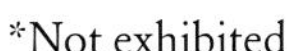

*Not exhibited

Published on the occasion of the exhibition

Mary Weatherford *The Flaying of Marsyas*

April 20–November 27, 2022

Museo di Palazzo Grimani
Castello 4858A
30122 Venezia
T. +39 041 241 1507

Ministry of Culture, Italy, and Museo di Palazzo Grimani
Director, State Museums of Veneto: Daniele Ferrara
Director, Museo di Palazzo Grimani: Valeria Finocchi

Venetian Heritage
Director: Toto Bergamo Rossi
Secretary General: Giorgio Ceccato
Press and external relations officer: Valentina Farace

Mary Weatherford Studio
Mollie White, Dustin Metz, Sandy Lu, Harley Eaves, Charles Moody, Harley Hollenstein, Timo Fahler, and Daniel Gibson

Gagosian
Project directors: Andrew Fabricant, Nick Simunovic, and Millicent Wilner
Senior director: Pepi Marchetti Franchi
Exhibition manager: Natasha Turk
Exhibition coordinators: Manuela Cúccuru and Antonello Martella
Chief creative officer: Alison McDonald
Director, Publications: Lauren Mahony
Director of external exhibitions: Adele Minardi
Print production manager: Shiori Kawasaki
Editorial assistant: Helen Redmond
Coordinators: Wyatt Allgeier, Madeline Amos, Elizabeth Chander, Brett Garde, Darlina Goldak, Olivia Mull, Elena Pinchiurri, Alanis Santiago-Rodriguez, Claudia Staccioli, and Andie Trainer
Text editor: David Frankel

WHY Architecture
Kulapat Yantrasast
Brian Butterfield
Mirtilla Alliata di Montereale

Marsilio Arte
Organizing director: Silvia Carrer
Exhibition manager: Carlotta Sapori
Communications officer: Chiara Pessina
Press consultant: Giovanni Sgrignuoli
Administrator: Valentina Maria Bertin
Bookshop and services coordination: Francesca Gennari

UNISVE
Guido Jaccarino and Katia Jancikic

NEONLAURO
Neon specialist: Raimondo Piaia

Delta Light and Baldieri Lighting Design
Lighting

Arterìa
Transportation

Jacket: Mary Weatherford, *The Flaying of Marsyas—Soft White and Sunrise* (2021–22; detail); see plate VI.

All photography by Fredrik Nilsen Studio except pp. 4–6: Library of Congress Geography and Map Division, Washington, DC, 20540-4650 USA dcu, call number G6714.V4 1729 .U4; p. 11: Zdeněk Sodoma, Muzeum umění Olomouc - Arcidiecézní muzeum Kroměříž (Olomouc Museum of Art - Archdiocesan Museum Kroměříž); p. 12 (top): © Saint Louis Art Museum/Bridgeman Images; p. 12 (bottom): Peter Horree/Alamy Stock Photo; p. 14 (top): Edward C. Robison III, courtesy Crystal Bridges Museum of American Art; p. 14 (bottom): Masur (talk|contribs)/Wikimedia Commons; pp. 18–31: Matteo D'Eletto, M3Studio

980 Madison Avenue
New York, NY 10075
T. +1 212.744.2313
gagosian.com

Distributed by Rizzoli International Publications
300 Park Avenue South
New York, NY 10010
rizzoliusa.com

Design by Graphic Thought Facility, London
Color separations by ArtProduct, Los Angeles
Printed by Pureprint Group, Uckfield, England

ISBN: 978-0-7893-4554-7
Library of Congress Control Number: 2023951425